The Whole-Life Pastor

I0895079

The Whole-Life Pastor

AN AUGUSTINIAN VISION FOR PASTORAL MINISTRY

MARK D. ALLEN

Baker Academic
a division of Baker Publishing Group
Grand Rapids, Michigan

Published by Baker Academic
a division of Baker Publishing Group
Grand Rapids, Michigan
BakerAcademic.com

Printed in the United States of America

Library of Congress Cataloging-in-Publication Data
Names: Allen, Mark D. (Mark Dwayne), 1961– author
Title: The whole-life pastor : an Augustinian vision for pastoral ministry / Mark D. Allen.
Description: Grand Rapids, Michigan : Baker Academic, a division of Baker Publishing Group, [2026] | Includes biographical information. | Includes bibliographical references and index.
Identifiers: LCCN 2026002787 | ISBN 9781540963635 paper | ISBN 9781493455737 ebook | ISBN 9781493455744 pdf
Subjects: LCSH: Pastoral theology—Catholic Church | Healing—Religious aspects—Christianity
Classification: LCC BX1913 .A575 2026
LC record available at https://lccn.loc.gov/2026002787

Cover design by Peter Gloege, LOOK | design studio

Baker Publishing Group publications use paper produced from sustainable forestry practices and postconsumer waste whenever possible.

26 27 28 29 30 31 32 7 6 5 4 3 2 1

For Colton, beloved son of the Father;
with you I am well pleased.

CONTENTS

ACKNOWLEDGMENTS

"Though busy with the realities of ministry and local leadership, Augustine always made time to discuss theology with his friends. In fact, he saw friendship as key to growth in Christlike virtue and theological growth," write Coleman Ford and Shawn Wilhite.[1]

Pastors are often busy people. Lately I have realized that I start my day—usually very early in the morning—with a feeling that I am behind and need to catch up. I have an intense sense of urgency to get things done. As I turn in to bed, I usually assess my day as good or bad based on how much I accomplished. At my age, I am trying to undo this relentless drive to achieve.

One of the major reasons that I am attempting to slow down is that in my efforts to complete my to-do list, I am tempted to reduce people to means for accomplishing my objectives rather than means of grace—the grace of theological and spiritual formation. My transactional encounters with people diminish my soul rather than expand it. My hurry often prevents me from experiencing the virtue-forming power of friendship.

That's why I appreciate the task of writing acknowledgments. The process slows me down to reflect on the people—the people they are, not just what they have done—who have shepherded me through this process. They have become friends who along the way have made me a better human and a better pastor.

First on my list are Josh Chatraw and Jack Carson, who have encouraged, inspired, and challenged me in my theological and literary development. I feel honored that they have included me in their relational world. Certainly they are true friends and sources of growth for my soul.

1. Ford and Wilhite, *Ancient Wisdom for the Care of Souls*, 152.

Let me add to the list my teaching fellow, Adebukola “Bukky” Adebayo, and my graduate assistant, Trinity Sailer, for their relentless devotion to me and my academic pursuits; my PhD students Matthew Hamilton, Michael Malcom, and Sungjoo Yoon, who read the manuscript and helped me believe that the book could make a positive difference in pastoral ministry; and my independent study MDiv students Joseph Dennis, Jorge Rivera-Marrero, Dennis Nicholson, and Elyse Penton, who critiqued an early version of the book and attended an ETS conference with me in San Diego to listen to me make a presentation on Augustine’s therapeutic preaching. Their discerning suggestions caused me to rearrange the order of the chapter on preaching. These are all beautiful people and wonderful friends who have shown me the shepherding grace and love of Jesus.

I would like to offer a special thanks to my friends in Christ at Memorial Methodist Church in Appomattox, Virginia. You have been a source of grace and healing to me. I could not have authored this book without you.

Thanks to my friend and pastor Tyler Scarlett of Forest Baptist Church, who modeled for me what a whole-life pastor looks like.

I am so grateful for the hours that my son, Colton, and I spent together poring over the manuscript in the summer of 2025—a rare privilege for a father and his son. Thanks to Colton for formatting my footnotes, developing the index and bibliography, correcting my grammar, and refining my prose, not to mention for his keen theological and ministerial insights.

Thanks to the three most wonderful women in my life: my wife, Karen, and two daughters, Katie and Jackie. In my pastoral ministry, you have endured much, showing grace and beauty at every turn. I love you.

Thank you to Dave Nelson and Anna Gissing. Thank you also to my acquisitions editor Dustyn Keepers, project editor Jenn Koenes, and the entire team at Baker Academic.

Thank you to these friends who have shepherded me through the process of writing *The Whole-Life Pastor*. May we continue to experience together—through our friendship—the healing grace of the shepherd and overseer of our souls, the Lord Jesus Christ.

INTRODUCTION

If we are to understand Augustine, we need . . . to hear him negotiating [the] frontier between pastoral instruction and theological vision.

—Rowan Williams, *On Augustine*

Augustine of Hippo suggested that the church was like a field hospital—full of wounded and ill people, who were recovering under the care of Christ the physician and the medicine that he provides.

—Alister McGrath, *Christian Apologetics*

And let me make it quite clear that when Christians say the Christ-life is in them, they do not mean simply something mental or moral. When they speak of being "in Christ" or of Christ being "in them," this is not simply a way of saying that they are thinking about Christ or copying Him. They mean that Christ is actually operating through them; that the whole mass of Christians are the physical organism through which Christ acts—that we are His fingers and muscles, the cells of His body.

—C. S. Lewis, *Mere Christianity*

Why This Book?

A couple weeks ago, my son, Colton, invited me to go to the newest Marvel movie: *Thunderbolts*. He had already seen it and wanted me to see it with him. Usually I can take or leave Marvel movies. I don't like them that much.

The biggest problem is I don't make an emotional connection with those movies.

Thunderbolts was different. This is the Marvel B team. The main characters are a bit rough around the edges. What I like best about the movie is that it goes explicitly after the depression, loneliness, sense of purposelessness, and depth of guilt that the emerging generation feels. I couldn't believe I was watching something so in touch with the angst of younger people and, for that matter, people today in general. It's probably no accident that the movie was released on May 1, the first day of Mental Health Awareness Month. The producers of the movie likely understand the brokenness and longings of people today. They get the need for companionship and for a purpose in life. They are in touch with the overwhelming guilt that so many people feel.

We live in a fragmented, convulsing world. People are saddened and separated. Shame, guilt, and regret press in on people every day. For many, life feels overwhelming and meaningless. The church has been affected by this cultural malaise—so has the pastor.

Biblical and gospel-centered pastoral ministry today must address cultural issues and take seriously the need for holistic healing. Ministry must include

- a way to experience solidarity, community, and unity;
- a vital spirituality that addresses our spiritual longings and integrates all aspects of our lives;
- an authentic way forward to increasing and lasting happiness without avoiding the harsh realities of life;
- a credible and established authority that helps us make decisions amid increasing complexity and make sense of our lives in an ever-changing world;
- a metastory that is not oppressive and exploitive but hopeful and uplifting for all;
- a path to overcome our guilt and shame and to move forward in a positive way toward a hopeful future;
- a therapeutic approach that takes our cultural and personal sin seriously; and
- a purposeful existence that is grounded in love.

This book equips pastors to minister to a world that needs and desires to be made whole in a time that calls for healing and hope.

Why Augustine?

"Remember, the exit door you're looking for may be behind you." This reminder is given thousands of times each day during safety instructions on airplanes across the world.[1] Perhaps the way out of our present cultural malaise is to look behind us to a fourth- and fifth-century bishop.

Yes, we look back to the ancient Augustine of Hippo, but in many ways, he is our contemporary, claims philosopher James K. A. Smith. Smith offers us another analogy: Like a boatman who faces one direction while rowing in another, we can move forward by looking backward. To move forward in pastoral ministry, we need Augustine in sight. Many cultural shapers of late modernity also kept Augustine in sight. A few examples include

- Martin Heidegger, who was a father of existentialism and unleashed our quest for authenticity;
- Albert Camus, who opened our imaginations to the absurdity, meaninglessness, and purposelessness of reality; and
- Jacques Derrida, who undermined our confidence in unchanging truths and showed us the logic of deconstructing many of our cherished beliefs.[2]

The whole Augustine can help us identify these culture shapers' influence and show us the problems with their partial appropriations of him. But we need the *whole* Augustine. By "the whole Augustine," I mean we must not forget what was most central to him: Jesus Christ, the Scriptures, and the church.[3] Yet Augustine is not just a cultural critic of late modern influencers. He understood the philosophical forces behind late modernity long before they became prominent and helps us capture these narratives within a larger, more expansive, holistic story. He anticipated them. Augustine truly is our contemporary.

Both Roman Catholics and Protestants proudly claim Augustine. One of my PhD colleagues and friends is John Sehorn. He is the dean of the graduate school of theology at the Augustine Institute, an influential Roman Catholic institution committed to the renewal of the church and the transformation of the world. Obviously, the members of the institute are fans of Augustine.

1. Timothy Paul Jones offers this wonderful analogy for retrieval in "Ecclesial Apologetics," 139.

2. J. K. A. Smith, *On the Road*, xiii, 20–21. See also J. K. A. Smith's *Who's Afraid of Postmodernism?*

3. As with the three examples above, there have been many secular receptions of Augustine that do not take seriously enough the deep structure of his pastoral theology.

They—like many other Roman Catholics—believe that Augustinianism is an important key to the renewal of the church. But evangelicals are raving fans of Augustine as well. I work at a huge evangelical university. Recently my wife and I walked into the university library to check out some books. The president of the university was standing at the door to the library, greeting potential football recruits. I walked over to him, stuck out my hand for a handshake, and introduced my wife and myself to him. I told him that I was doing research for and writing a book on Augustine. Immediately he became inquisitive. His passion for Augustine was obvious.

Why Augustine? His pastoral theology relates to Christians across the denominational spectrum. No matter what tradition you are located in, Augustine will have something to say to you. Augustine has shaped Christianity—and the world, for that matter—as much as anyone who has lived since his pastoral ministry in North Africa.

Yet I desire to share Augustine with you because of the transformation he has caused on my life and ministry. I began researching Augustine in earnest in preparation for a book that Josh Chatraw and I coauthored on Augustine's approach to apologetics, *The Augustine Way: Retrieving a Vision for the Church's Apologetic Witness*. While researching and writing, I sensed a need for a book on the way Augustine's theology—particularly his Christology, ecclesiology, bibliology, anthropology, and eschatology—shaped his pastoral ministry. In this book, I try to share how he has changed my pastoral ministry and suggest ways that he might help you minister to your congregation in the complex world we live in.

One of my editors for this book made his thoughts on retrieving Augustine clear to me: "I want more of you in this book than of Augustine." I felt flattered, but I think what he was saying is this: "I want you to speak to pastoral ministry today. Do not leave Augustine in the fifth century. Bring him up to today. I want to hear your pastoral voice."

He wanted me to speak out of my own experiences in pastoral ministry. That's why I tell so many personal and pastoral stories in this book. It contains many of my own personal "confessions." This book is about how Augustine can speak to pastoral ministry today. To retrieve him, I had to receive him into my own past and present ministry and ask myself how he could have helped me when I first started and how he can shape my ministry now. I hope that many who read this book feel that my personal illustrations illuminate Augustine's profound theology and that my reflections on his pastoral ministry prove valuable for their own appropriation of this ancient saint's ministry.

Yet even though there are many personal reflections and experiences in the book, I quote Augustine often. Very often. Why? Because I want readers to hear Augustine's voice for themselves. It's amazing how profoundly and directly this fourth- and fifth-century saint speaks to our twenty-first-century ministry. I desire for you to hear for yourself Augustine's pastoral heart. So I have done the heavy lifting for you. I have pored over many of the works of Augustine and have given you "the best" of Augustine's pastoral perspectives and ministry. At least, these are the quotes that have been the most inspiring and relevant to my pastoral formation. I encourage you to let him speak directly to your ministry as well.

Further, I quote scholars often. I bring a chorus of scholars to the table. Why? I want you to witness the pastoral and spiritual instincts of academics who hunger for God and the church. I desire to share with you the riches of academic scholarship and theology for pastoral ministry. Enrich yourself through reading their very words. Drink deep from the depth of their reflections and insights.

A Warning

This book does not sit comfortably in any one tradition. There's something here for every Christian tradition to embrace and something for every Christian tradition to reject. I have attempted to write *The Whole-Life Pastor* to fit comfortably within the Great Tradition, but not every tradition.

My own spiritual and pastoral formation has occurred within the wide pastures of the Great Tradition. I am a catholic Christian with a Baptist heritage.

Recently, after serving for six years as a lay elder in a Southern Baptist church, I received a call to pastor a Methodist church in a nearby town. I accepted the call and was sent out by the congregation with their blessing. One Sunday, the pastor of the Baptist church where I had served as an elder surprised me by showing up for our morning service. After his visit, he wrote in his church bulletin about his experience:

> The congregation was everything Mark had described. They have a beautiful facility. Even in just one visit, I can say that Memorial Methodist seems to be a warm fellowship of believers who love God's word, God's Son and God's people.
>
> The worship service was one of the most diverse I have ever experienced. It was, as I told my wife, "soooo Mark Allen." If you know Mark, he is a lover and advocate for the Great Tradition, or faithful Christian expression across history and denominations. And Memorial's service reflected it beautifully. In addition to the normal sermon and singing, there was a reciting of the Apostle's Creed, a responsive reading from the Psalms, the Lord's Supper (by intinction), robes, candles and silence. There were even Jewish elements (the service began

> with the blowing of the shofar or ram's horn) and Irish elements (the service ended with a Celtic blessing in song). I felt like I experienced the best of twelve different denominations in one worship service. The Baptist got his "liturgy fix" for a while.
>
> I am happy to report that Mark seems to be in his element.[4]

That is my element. But that is not everyone's element. Even in my Baptist pastor's reflection on the service, he labeled some parts of our worship "normal." By implication, other parts were not "normal," or at least, part of his Baptist tradition. My advice to the reader is to chew on the meat and spit out the bones. Receive what you can into your tradition. Modify it. Edit out what runs counter to your ministry context. Throughout his ministry, Augustine remained nimble—under the authority of Scripture, the mediation of Jesus Christ, and the oversight of his church—growing and responding holistically to diverse pastoral circumstances on the ground.

An Overview of the Book

Augustine was a pastor theologian par excellence.[5] He did his theology in the context of pastoral ministry. He was intensely practical. His theology grew out of his life as a pastor and was a response to the needs of his church. Rowan Williams affirms this perspective on Augustine's theological formation: "Augustine's theological exposition is seldom systematic; we have to work with him and follow the connections he makes. And yet such labour at least clarifies the inseparability of these themes [the doctrines of grace, of Christ, of signs and sacraments and a practice of self-scrutinizing humility expressed in psalmodic prayer] in what he writes and preaches, and warns against the abstraction of his doctrine from his pastoring."[6]

As a pastor theologian, Augustine was a "whole-life pastor." He integrated all aspects of life into his pastoral ministry. Recently a new attendee at our church who has explored various lifestyles asked me, "Pastor, do you think God wants to be involved in all aspects of our lives?" (He had no idea that

4. Church bulletin, Forest Baptist Church, Forest, VA, January 14, 2024.

5. In 2015 a couple books that cast a vision for the integration of theology and pastoral ministry were published: *The Pastor Theologian: Resurrecting an Ancient Vision* by Gerald Hiestand and Todd Wilson, and *The Pastor as Public Theologian: Reclaiming a Lost Vision* by Kevin J. Vanhoozer and Owen Strachan. Both books emphasize the importance of being a pastor theologian. I hope this book advances the practicality of being a pastor who integrates theology into all aspects of ministry.

6. Williams, *On Augustine*, 37.

I was writing a book titled *The Whole-Life Pastor*.) I answered yes. I think Augustine would have taken this perspective as well.

We long to be whole—whole pastors who shepherd whole churches with whole people living in whole stories and walking the whole journey. In what follows I overview how I develop this thesis.

Part 1: The Whole Christ

Chapter 1: Uniting the Church

Chapter 1 introduces the significant pastoral implications of Augustine's "whole-Christ" teaching. This chapter defines the whole Christ, advocates that this christological and ecclesial theology has unifying and healing pastoral power, and addresses some of the worries that Augustine's whole-Christ teaching raises.

The whole-Christ teaching is a mystical and ecclesial theology that recognizes the oneness of the head and the body. Jesus Christ has chosen to unite himself to his people in such a way that he is their head and they are members of his body. Jesus Christ as head and the church as body together form the whole Christ. The chapter ends by raising the practical question "How can pastors start implementing the whole-Christ ecclesiology in a healing and unifying way?"

Chapter 2: Praying the Psalms

In chapter 2, we see Augustine's transformative vision for praying the Psalms as the whole Christ. In praying the Psalms together, we discover ourselves, our common humanity, and our life in Christ. We are united in Christ, and he intercedes for us. We enter a solidarity of suffering and healing through praying the Psalms as the whole Christ. Jesus Christ, our mediator, heals us as we pray the Psalms for ourselves and for one another. Christ shepherds the sheep of our congregations through these prayers.

Part 2: The Whole Person

Chapter 3: Loving Administration

Chapter 3 introduces Augustine's holistic anthropology. For him, people must believe to understand. Also, for Augustine, humans are primarily lovers—lovers who believe and think. We pastor integrated people: not just believers, not just thinkers, not just lovers, but lovers who believe in order to understand.

From another holistic perspective, we humans have affections, will, and cognition. The affections direct the will to the object of our love. When our will is directed toward the proper love—God—our minds are open to understand the truth about who he is. We are loving, choosing, learning beings. These aspects of our personhood are deeply connected, but love is the beginning and end of who we are.

In this chapter, I will show how Augustinian holistic anthropology affects our daily administrative tasks. Administration is more than getting things done in an efficient and orderly way. As we manage a church, the aim and motivation should be love. We ask ourselves, "How can every administrative task be motivated by love and grow love?"

Chapter 4: Preaching That Heals

Chapter 4 will focus on preaching as a therapeutic act. Augustine's emphasis on the whole Christ and his view of holistic anthropology can transform the way we preach. The various aspects of the worship service (sacraments, prayers, creeds, confessions, singing) and the heart of the preacher (their prayer life, humility, and saturation in Scripture) join to bring healing to the hurting. The church is a hospital for ailing sinners. Jesus Christ is the medic and the medicine. In Christ and his church, preaching can be an act of healing.

Part 3: The Whole Story

Chapter 5: Fortifying the Fragilized

In chapter 5, we see how Augustine shepherded a flock whose faith had been fragilized: Some had walked away from the Christian faith, others were shaky in their faith, and still others had never believed in the first place. From Augustine's pastoral approach four questions emerge: (1) What story are you living in? (2) What are you seeking? (3) What authority are you living under? (4) What community is forming you? Building these questions into the church's evangelistic and discipleship life can help congregants have a more authentic faith—a fortified and flourishing faith that relates to all aspects of their personal and interpersonal lives.

Chapter 6: Persuading Skeptics

Chapter 6 applies the apologetic methodology of Augustine's *The City of God* to today's cultural context. Augustine enters his challengers' cultural story, critiques it, and retells it within the biblical narrative. Augustine aims to convert the culture and those inhabiting the culture to Christianity's better story. Using the Augustinian Inside Out methodology, pastors will learn how to train their congregations in an effective apologetic methodology. The apologetic applications are personal and relational but also prepare the church to engage wider contemporary issues.

Part 4: The Whole Journey

Chapter 7: Living in Public Spaces

Chapter 7 presents an Augustinian public theology. It aims to equip pastors to train congregants to live in public spaces. Augustine views life as a way, a journey homeward. Through their teaching and preaching, pastors guide their parishioners to take the next steps upward. Step-by-step, upward and onward, the congregation advances homeward. As Jesus Christ came down to take us up with himself, the pastor relates the Scriptures to where people are to enable them to take their next step upward. The church body—the whole Christ—is on a hopeful pilgrimage. On pilgrimage homeward, the whole Christ brings the future blessings to bear in public spaces in the here and now. The church seeks to bring some of what will be to what is. The church shares the goods of the world to come for the common good of public life in the world today.

Now let's go on a journey with the whole-life pastor.

PART ONE

The Whole Christ

ONE

Uniting the Church

This is the highest honour of the Church, that, until He is united to us, the Son of God reckons himself in some measure imperfect. What consolation is it for us to learn, that, not until we are along with him, does he possess all his parts, or wish to be regarded as complete! Hence, in the First Epistle to the Corinthians, when the apostle discusses largely the metaphor of a human body, he includes under the single name of Christ the whole Church.

—John Calvin, *Commentaries on the Epistles of Paul to the Galatians and Ephesians*

The Spirit of God flows through Christ into the whole of his true Church, permeating every part of his wonderful mystical body; but the Spirit of God is first on the Head, and in the Head, and then from him the gracious unction of the Holy One descends to the entire body.

—Charles Spurgeon, "The Head and the Body"

The pastor stands at the back of the church. It's five minutes before the beginning of the Sunday morning worship service. His eyes scan the congregation. Some attendees smile warmly as they move from row to row greeting their fellow church members. Others sequester themselves with their families and sit in silence. A few have chosen a seat a safe distance from others, where they can withdraw and attempt to avoid eye contact. The empty seats await those latecomers who will slide in just after the service starts.

But the pastor knows too much; all is not as it appears. From years of pastoral ministry, he can feel the thickness of the air and the heaviness in the room. The same-sex-attracted twentysomething. The entrepreneur finally admitting that his business is going under. The recent college graduate drowning in $80,000 of debt and bemoaning the reality that he can't get a decent job. The small group leader hungering for God but perpetually feeling distant from him. The spry fiftysomething who was stunned last week when his doctor used the C-word. The high-achieving professional fueled by her desperation to prove her worth to her father. The deacon struggling to remain faithful to a wife who hasn't let him touch her in three years. The assistant pastor whose adult son informed him last month that he is deconstructing his faith. The grandparents barred from seeing their grandkids because their Christian faith has been labeled dangerous. The Sunday school teacher who hasn't prayed in years because of her disappointment with God.

One by one, like one brick stacked on another, the sorrow and pain of each individual weighs heavily on him. Anger. Lust. Loneliness. Greed. Guilt. Resentment. Confusion. Depression. Vanity. Disappointment. Fear. Worry. Restlessness. Shame. Denial. Pride. Selfishness. The room is thick with these maladies—thick because these issues compound whenever the members relate to one another. The pastor knows the terms for analyzing and fixing corporate dysfunction: "triangulation," "enmeshment," "homeostasis," "family secrets," "identified patient," "nonanxious presence," and so on. He could write a book on family systems and church health. But then again, books are hard to write, and even more difficult to practice.

Then there are the expectations that his parishioners lay on him and, perhaps worse, those he places on himself. In the early days of his ministry, he considered himself better than those other struggling pastors. He would be able to meet and exceed expectations that other pastors could not—and God would help him do it. Those days are over. Now he feels more like an overwhelmed father carrying many bags of groceries that suddenly burst and scatter across the garage floor. It's so hard for him to keep himself together, but it's even more difficult to keep a church with so many diverse expectations together. He has fallen far short of the standards he set for himself. And he is a long way from living up to the cumulative expectations his congregation has for him: funeral director, wedding planner, strategist, vision caster, mission leader, marketeer, administrator, real-estate developer, facilities project manager, maintenance director, preacher, motivational speaker, chaplain, therapist, community organizer, prayer warrior, faith healer, Bible scholar, evangelist. He thinks that he should somehow fulfill their expectations. Or more introspectively, he thinks he should worry more about their real pain than about his own limitations. The real issue is that they need genuine healing and transformation—and so does he.

To add another layer on all this, cultural forces outside the room threaten to fracture the brotherhood and sisterhood in the room. On a weekly basis, these people inhabit an increasingly fragmented world. The Christian Scriptures no longer hold sway over the cultural narrative the way they once did. With the rise of expressive individualism ("You do you" and "Chase your dream") and the ethics of authenticity ("Live your truth"), pluralism has been radicalized and faith, fragilized. Today, there are as many stories—and religions, for that matter—as there are individuals.

Strong currents rage throughout the culture, sucking individual swimmers into their pull and sometimes crashing the collective groups into one another with the thrust of religious fervor. There's the current of wokeness and self-care, the current of utopian technology with its reimagined self, the current of revived masculinity and the natural order. These are the remixed religious waters the congregants flail in every day with their "strange rites" of spiritual healing, apocalyptic visions, and warrior zeal.[1] Talk radio, social media, podcasts, and cable news have tribalized these currents and imbued them with the passion of religious fundamentalism. The attendees sit in their seats on this Sunday morning fractured by the push and pull of these titanic cultural currents. Their world is convulsing, yet many sit oblivious to the toll that all this angry divisiveness is taking on their souls.

With these currents running right through the aisles of the church, the pastor wonders if in the world today the church can ever be united and healed. To make matters even more complicated, for centuries various conflicting streams have flowed through the universal church, working themselves out in local churches: Catholics versus Protestants; charismatics versus cessationists; pedobaptizers versus credobaptizers; memorialists versus sacramentalists; Calvinists versus Arminians; Anabaptists versus Theonomists; amillennialists versus premillennialists; High Churchers versus Low Churchers; egalitarians versus complementarians; contemporary versus traditional; Anglicans, Presbyterians, Methodists, Baptists, Assemblies of God, and Independents versus one another. Sometimes the strong and diverse opinions over debatable issues feel like ticking time bombs that could suddenly blow up and split his church into angry factions.

In his young and optimistic days, the pastor felt confident that he would be able to unite a congregation. Surely through his strategic vision, his strong pastoral gifts, his expositional preaching, and his vibrant spiritual life he would be able to influence crowds of people to join one another in a united mission. Others had seemed to do it; surely he could do it too. He was called,

1. Burton, *Strange Rites*.

went to the right seminary, attended the right conferences, read the right books, and was ready to change the world. Then reality set in. People are fallen and broken. They are hard to please and even harder to unite, at least in any substantive way. Recently, through some serious introspection, he has come to realize that he had hoped to unite them around, well, himself. Fortunately for him and the church—though he hasn't felt fortunate under the circumstances—he has come to the end of himself and his confidence in his ability to unite this suffering and fragmented congregation. But he has not come to the end of his love for them and his longing to see them experience healing and live in solidarity with one another.

As he steps toward the platform, he thinks, "Perhaps a better pastor could unite this church and lead them on a journey toward healing."

Augustine's Whole-Christ Teaching

You Did It for Me?

In this chapter, I suggest that the whole Christ is the better pastor.

What, or perhaps who, is the "whole Christ"? The whole Christ, or in Latin, *totus Christus*, is an ecclesiological proposal that begins with Jesus Christ. As I mentioned above, Christ has chosen to unite himself to his people in such a way that he is their head and they are members of his body. Jesus Christ as head and the church as body together form the whole Christ.

Augustine reminded his congregation often about the significance of the whole Christ. He grounded his doctrine of totus Christus primarily in two texts: Acts 9:4–5 and Matthew 25:31–46. One prime example of this grounding is found in a sermon given on a feast of the martyrs in 411. He urges the congregation toward indifference concerning the things of this world, particularly riches. He admonishes his listeners to bank their treasures in heaven by giving their riches to Christ. If they give their treasures to Christ on earth, they are depositing them in a secure heavenly place and will receive them back richly up there.

With his usual rhetorical flair, Augustine imagines his congregation's objections: "'Yes,' you say, 'but where do I find Christ? . . . He is seated at the right hand of the Father, he is going to come again at the end. When can I find him here? To whom can I give?'"[2]

"Well I am glad you asked!" Augustine replies. He first responds by calming his congregation's worries: "Stop fretting; listen to the whole of it." He

2. Augustine, *Sermons* 345.4.

then reminds them of Paul's bloodthirsty persecution of the church and his encounter with Christ: "You've heard, haven't you, what the one who, as you confess, is seated in heaven cried out to him?"[3] Augustine helps them call to mind what they have heard and read:

> *Saul, Saul, why are you persecuting me?* (Acts 9:1–4). Paul, I mean to say, could neither see him nor touch him; and yet he said to him, *Why are you persecuting me?* He didn't say, "Why are you persecuting my family, my servants, my saints"—add another title of honor—"my brothers and sisters." Nothing of that sort. But what did he say? *Why are you persecuting me?* That is, my members, on whose behalf, as they were being trampled upon on earth, the head was crying out from heaven. Because even for your own foot, when it's trodden upon on the ground, your tongue doesn't cry out, "You're treading on my foot," but "You're treading on me."[4]

Augustine then relates this general totus Christus teaching—the head and the members together make up the whole Christ—to his specific point of giving riches to Christ here on earth: "So why have any doubts about whom you can give to? It's the one who said, *Saul, Saul, why are you persecuting me?* It's the same one who says to you, 'Feed me on earth.' Saul was raging, and yet it was Christ that he was persecuting." Augustine explains that the Lord knew that those who would ultimately be set to his right hand would be bothered by the question while on earth, so Augustine clarifies, "When [Jesus] says, *I was hungry and you gave me to eat*, they will reply, *Lord, when did we see you hungry?* And straightaway they will hear, *When you did it for one of these least of mine, you did it for me* (Mt 25:35–40)."[5]

Jesus Christ, the head of the church, who is seated in heaven, so identifies with his church that he can speak of it as "me." He freely claims, "You persecute the church; you persecute me. You feed and clothe the church; you feed and clothe me." The head and the body together are the whole Christ.

In an earlier sermon preached in Carthage, Augustine asserts the deep unity and shared identity between Christ and his church: "Now, however, I wonder if we shouldn't have a look at ourselves, if we shouldn't think about his body, because he is also us. . . . So we too are him, because we are his organs, because we are his body, because he is our head, because the whole Christ is both head and body."[6] Christ is for us, with us, and in us. In our struggles and sins, Christ is in us, both suffering with us and redeeming us.

3. Augustine, *Sermons* 345.4.
4. Augustine, *Sermons* 345.4 (italics original).
5. Augustine, *Sermons* 345.4 (italics original).
6. Augustine, *Sermons* 133.8.

The Body and the Bride

Augustine also builds his whole-Christ teaching on the church as the body of Christ and the bride of Christ. In Augustine's totus Christus teaching, Jesus Christ's connection with his church goes beyond a mere external identification. Through the Holy Spirit, Jesus Christ is united with his church and his church is united with him; he participates in his church and his church participates in him. The fellowship, produced by the Holy Spirit, between Christ and his church is so profound that Augustine uses the surprising nomenclature "whole Christ" to emphasize the depth of unity between the head and the body, husband and bride.

Using the biblical metaphors of body and bride, Augustine demonstrates both the deep unity between the body and its head and the appropriate distinction between the bridegroom and the bride. The body and the bride join into one body, yet they are two. Augustine explains that in Scripture we must understand Christ in three ways: as (1) the Word equal to the Father, (2) the incarnate Word as our mediator, and (3) the whole Christ, which is bride and bridegroom joined together in one body, the church.

> Head and body form one Christ. Not that he isn't complete without the body, but that he was prepared to be complete together with us as well, though even without us he is always complete. . . . All the same, brothers and sisters, how are we his body, and he one Christ with us? Where do we find this, that head and body form one Christ, that is, the body together with its head? In Isaiah he is speaking as if in the singular, and it's one and the same person speaking; and see what is said: *As for a bridegroom he has bound a turban on my head, and as for a bride he has decked me out with ornaments* (Is 61:10). As bridegroom and bride: he calls one and the same person bridegroom with reference to the head, bride with reference to the body. There seem to be two, and there's one.[7]

Like a bridegroom and bride who are joined together as one flesh and yet remain two separate individuals, Jesus Christ and his church are united into one body—the whole Christ—yet remain distinct from each other.

The Holy Spirit and Charity

The many parts of the body of Christ are individual and unique but are joined together by the Holy Spirit. In 412, some in Augustine's congregation were worried that they might not have received the Holy Spirit because they had not spoken in tongues. In a sermon delivered on the day of Pentecost,

7. Augustine, *Sermons* 341.19 (Dolbeau 22).

Augustine explains to them that not all speak in tongues; the united body has many parts:

> Our spirit, by which every person lives, is called the soul. . . . And you can see what the soul does in the body. It quickens all its parts; it sees through the eyes, hears through the ears, smells through the nostrils, speaks with the tongue, works with the hands, walks with the feet. It's present simultaneously to all the body's parts, to make them alive; it gives life to all, their functions to each. The eye doesn't hear, the ear doesn't see, the tongue doesn't see, nor do ear and eye speak. But they're alive, all the same; the ear's alive, the tongue's alive; different functions, life in common. . . . What the soul is to the human body, the Holy Spirit is to the body of Christ, which is the Church. The Holy Spirit does in the whole Church what the soul does in all the parts of one body.[8]

The Holy Spirit draws Christians "closer to God and one another in mutual love."[9] He unites otherwise disparate and fragmented people—like those in the congregation in the introduction to this chapter—together in love.

Augustine counsels his listeners that if they want to be alive with the Holy Spirit, then they must live in the Holy Spirit's gift of charity: "Hold on to loving-kindness, love truthfulness, long for oneness, that you may attain to everlastingness."[10] Charity draws the people of God together: "[Augustine] explained that the bond of charity was the unifying and life-giving principle of the Whole Christ, head and members."[11] The head and the body and all the individual members of the body live in solidarity through the Holy Spirit's love. They live united in this love as each member does their part to build up the others in love.

Trinitarian Love

This unifying love, wrought by the Spirit, draws the body together into trinitarian love:

> If by approaching God many souls become one soul through charity, and many hearts one heart, what is the very fount of charity doing in the Father and the Son? In that way, is not the Trinity even more one God? After all, charity comes to us from there, from the Holy Spirit, as the apostle says, *The charity of God has been poured out in our hearts through the Holy Spirit who has been given*

8. Augustine, *Sermons* 267.4.
9. Burns, *Augustine's Preached Theology*, 281.
10. Augustine, *Sermons* 267.4.
11. Burns, *Augustine's Preached Theology*, 281.

> *to us* (Rom 5:5). If, therefore, *the charity of God is poured out in our hearts through the Holy Spirit who has been given us*, making many souls into one soul, many hearts into one heart, how much more are Father and Son and Holy Spirit one God, one Light, one Beginning?[12]

As the whole Christ, the church has entered deep solidarity with the Holy Trinity, bound together in Christ by the Holy Spirit and united through charity.

The Whole Christ and the Sacraments

As Eve was created from the side of Adam as he slept, so the church was created from the side of Jesus in his sleep of death on the cross; thus argues Augustine. From Jesus's side flowed the sacraments—the water and the blood—which formed the church, the whole Christ.[13] In *Augustine and the Mystery of the Church*, James K. Lee explains, "The sacraments are intrinsic to the building up of the church and the formation of the whole Christ. . . . In his mature ecclesiology, the church is a communal body united in charity by means of the sacraments in order to form the whole Christ."[14]

Most obviously and importantly, the pastor makes the local congregation more aware of their real union with Christ and the church universal by connecting totus Christus with baptism and the Eucharist. "Augustine taught that the sacraments of baptism and eucharist signified the same religious good, though in different ways. The reality symbolized by each was membership in the body of the Whole Christ."[15] Baptism symbolizes the reality of incorporation into the whole Christ; the Eucharist symbolizes the spiritual presence of the "body of the Whole Christ, head and members, in which the faithful were already living."[16] The unifying reality of totus Christus becomes powerful in the consciousness of the Christian when it is connected to baptism and the Eucharist.

This is not to say that the sacraments are *mere* symbols, but they are vitally and spiritually significant in forming and enlivening the church.[17] The pastor must not put all the pressure of the ministry on himself. Through the invitation to partake of the sacraments, the church is grown and nourished in love. In *The Care of Souls: Cultivating a Pastor's Heart*, Harold L. Senkbeil

12. Augustine, *Homilies on the Gospel of John* 39.5 (italics original).

13. Augustine, *Expositions of the Psalms* 138.2.

14. Lee, *Augustine and the Mystery of the Church*, 28–29.

15. Burns, *Augustine's Preached Theology*, 126.

16. Burns, *Augustine's Preached Theology*, 119.

17. For a Baptist perspective on recovering the sacraments, see Haykin, *Amidst Us Our Beloved Stands*.

emphasizes the importance of the sacraments in pastoral ministry: "By our Lord's own mandate, he has so arranged it in his church that we grow, are fed, nourished, guarded, and protected not out of the weakness and ineptitude of our ministers but rather by the tools Christ has entrusted into their hands. The gospel and the sacraments are not static entities—mere object lessons by which we advertise and promote the kingdom of God. Rather, the gospel and sacraments throb with vitality. They are filled to the brim with the energy and life of God's own Spirit."[18] Again, Lee stresses the vital connection between the whole Christ and the sacraments: "The sacraments have been instituted in order to build up the church as the body of Christ. . . . The one body of Christ is 'built up' . . . by the sacraments until the final completion of the whole Christ."[19] The preaching of the gospel and the giving and receiving of the sacraments form and nurture the whole Christ.

Totus Christus Worries

Amid a fragmented church and divided world, the whole Christ offers hope for pastors, even if—or perhaps, especially if—they have come to the end of themselves and their ability to unite a church. It's not their personality, their vision, their strategy, or their eloquence that coalesces the congregation. Instead, the Holy Spirit brings the members into trinitarian love and works through charity to heal and unify the congregation.

Augustine's totus Christus teaching has the potential to unite and heal the church and to enlarge its witness. Yet you may have some questions about it, perhaps even some concerns about the doctrine's potential for some significant unintended consequences. You are not alone in your worries; some others in the church have raised concerns about Augustine's whole-Christ teaching.[20] But Augustine was not caught off guard by these worries. He addresses some directly and others implicitly in his preaching and teaching. Let's pause for a

18. Senkbeil, *Care of Souls*, 30.

19. Lee, *Augustine and the Mystery of the Church*, 44.

20. For an entrance into those worries, see the articles in the totus Christus symposium in *Pro Ecclesia*: Moser, "*Totus Christus*"; Vanhoozer, "Hocus Totus"; Horton, "Affirming Moser's Well-Qualified *Totus Christus*"; Michael Allen, "*Totus Christus* and Praying the Psalms"; Moser, "Corpus Mysticum." Notably, Vanhoozer admits in his predominantly critical article on totus Christus, "I am not saying, then, that every use of the *Totus Christus* necessarily leads to dogmatic disorder, only that its ambiguous reference may inadvertently produce such disorder" ("Hocus Totus," 32). Horton concludes his paper, "I also share [J. David Moser's] hopes that *Totus Christus*, the mystical union and related themes will receive the attention they have in our [Reformed] tradition in the past but seem somewhat to be too slightly contemplated today" ("Affirming Moser's Well-Qualified *Totus Christus*," 44).

bit to take an honest look at totus Christus worries and how Augustine helps us respond to these questions.

Has the Church Joined with Jesus Christ as the Second Member of the Trinity?

If Jesus Christ and the church together are the whole Christ, then is the church related to the Trinity the way Christ is? That is, if the church is one person with Jesus Christ, then has the church become one of the persons of the Trinity? Further, is the church the continuation of the incarnation of Jesus Christ?

Totus Christus does not require that the church and Christ become one the way the three persons of the Trinity are united or the way the two natures of Christ are hypostatically connected. Augustine emphasizes that the head (Christ) and the body (the church) are united into one body—through the work of the Holy Spirit—but he also acknowledges that the church and Christ are not united hypostatically in the same way as Christ's divine nature and human nature. Commenting with reference to Augustine's preaching, J. Patout Burns Jr. recognizes this distinction: "Augustine was conscious of significant differences between the union of divine and human in the Savior and the union of head and members in the Whole Christ."[21]

The church depends on Christ, but Christ does not depend on the church; Christ has an independent existence from the church. In his second exposition of Psalm 30, Augustine, commenting on 1 Corinthians 12:12, distinguishes between Christ and the members of his body while retaining their deep connection:

> A body is one single unit, with many members, but all the members of the body, numerous as they are, constitute one body; and it is the same with Christ. Many members, one body: Christ. All of us together with our Head are Christ, and without our Head we are helpless. Why? Because united with our Head we are the vine, but if cut off from our Head (God forbid!) we are only loppings, of no use to the vine-tenders and fit only for the bonfire. This is why Christ himself says in the gospel, *I am the vine, you are the branches, and my Father is the vine-dresser*; and he warns us, *Without me you can do nothing* (Jn 15:5.1). If we can achieve nothing without you, Lord, we can do everything in you. Yes, because whatever work he does through us seems to be our work. He can do plenty, or rather everything, without us, but we can do nothing without him.[22]

21. Burns, *Augustine's Preached Theology*, 262.
22. Augustine, *Expositions of the Psalms* 30.2.4 (italics original).

Christ and his church are one, yet Christ is independent from the church. He can work independently and freely without the church. In contrast, the church will cease to exist without Christ. Further, Christ can do everything without the church, but the church can do nothing without Christ.[23] The Holy Trinity and the incarnate Christ in his connection with the Trinity self-exist; the church does not self-exist. The church is not one of the persons of the Trinity.

In another sermon, dated 416, Augustine further explains the implications of John 15:5 for his whole-Christ teaching:

> In the same way, he also says to his disciples, *Because without me you can do nothing* (Jn 15:5). You see, he is one with the Father in one way, and one with us in quite another. He is one with the Father, because there is one substance of the Father and the Son. He is one with the Father, because *while he was in the form of God, he did not think it robbery to be equal to God*. But he became one with us, or rather one of us, because *he emptied himself, taking the form of a servant* (Phil 2:7).[24]

David Vincent Meconi clarifies that for Augustine, in the totus Christus, Christ remains divine, and the church remains human: "The Son of God may have become human so humans may become one with God, but that does not mean that humans will become God the same way the Son is God. . . . In this creaturely communion with the divine, we see how the *totus Christus* is always a matter of solidarity and dissimilarity: one with Christ in his will, yet other than Christ in his divinity."[25]

In 394 or 395, while Augustine was still serving as a priest, he left no doubt that the church has not taken on the divine nature in the way Christ did in his incarnation:

> It is by *putting on Christ* through faith that all are made sons—not by nature (as is the case with the only Son, who is indeed the Wisdom of God), and not by superior power or a unique assumption, accomplished in order to have and perform the role of Wisdom naturally. (Such was the case with the Mediator himself, who has been made one with the very Wisdom that assumed him without the interposition of any mediator). Rather, we are made sons by participation in Wisdom, with faith in the Mediator preparing and paving the way for it.[26]

23. Moser, "*Totus Christus*," 17.
24. Augustine, *Sermons* 144.5 (italics original).
25. Meconi, *One Christ*, 213.
26. Plumer, *Augustine's Commentary on Galatians*, 173 (italics original).

Does the church, as the whole Christ, continue the incarnation?[27] If we mean that the church's union with Christ is a hypostatic union like that of Christ's incarnation, then no! In that case, the church is not a continuation of the incarnation. Burns ends a chapter titled "Christ and the Church" in his *Augustine's Preached Theology* with this sentence: "[The whole Christ] points to a union that is more than voluntary but not fully physical, much less 'hypostatic.'"[28] Jesus refers to the church as "me" (Acts 9:4), and through the church, he continues what he began to do in his first advent (Acts 1:1). But there is more to Jesus Christ—as he reigns from heaven—than the church alone.[29]

In sum, the church has not joined Christ as the second member of the Trinity, and the church has not been joined to Christ in a second hypostatic union. Yet we have been united to Christ and to the Holy Trinity in deep solidarity through the Holy Spirit and the love he pours out into our hearts.

The second worry is related but has a different nuance.

Does Totus Christus Violate the Creator/Created Distinction?

Does totus Christus collapse Christ and the church into a single being so that both lose their distinctiveness? Further, since Christ is in heaven, is it impossible for him to be directly present in history among his human beings? Can the incarnate creator on his heavenly throne dwell physically among his creatures?

Indeed, Jesus Christ dwells in his church on earth (Col. 1:27), and his church is seated with him in heavenly places (Eph. 2:6). This mysterious union occurs through the Holy Spirit (1 Cor. 12:12–14). The head and his body are united with each other through their shared life in the Holy Spirit. Jesus Christ's

27. "Continuation" terminology is possible—in my seminary training, pastoral-ministries professors would encourage the church to engage in "incarnational" ministry, which to me seems helpful. Yes, we are the "hands and feet" of Christ.

28. Burns, *Augustine's Preached Theology*, 284.

29. John Webster clarifies what it means for the church to be "with" Christ:

> The church is indeed "made alive together with Christ"; it is "raised up with him," it "sits" with him in the heavenly places (Eph. 2.5f.). This "with Christ" has ontological weight: the church has its being with him. But what is the force of this "with"? It indicates an intimacy of relation between Christ the Lord and those whom he exalts to share his location, but one in which he retains his free, sovereign incommunicable identity. His co-location with the church is not such that his identity as the exalted Son becomes porous, or that he is no longer gracious towards the community. The church adds nothing to the identity of the exalted Son. "By grace" (Eph. 2.5, 8) is not merely the means of the church's entry into union with Christ but the permanent characteristic of that union, and therefore a signifier that the church's relation to its Lord is characterized by ever greater dissimilarity. (*God Without Measure*, 185–86)

physical body is in heaven, but he dwells in us and we in him through the Spirit of God. In the Holy Spirit, though our physical bodies remain essentially distinct, head (Christ) and body (church) are the whole Christ on earth.

However, the creator and the creature have not been collapsed into a single entity so that there is no longer a distinction between the two. Again, "he can do plenty, or rather everything, without us, but we can do nothing without him."[30] Jesus Christ can exist without the church, but the church cannot exist without Christ. The two are distinct but joined through the Holy Spirit. Further, there is a physicality to Jesus Christ's presence on the earth currently through the church, but he, in his physical body, remains a separate entity in heaven.

In a sermon dated 400, Augustine makes the creator/created distinction clear:

> Now to convince you that bride and bridegroom are one person with reference to the flesh of Christ, not to his divinity—after all, with respect to divinity we cannot be what he is, because he is creator we are creatures, he the maker we what he made, he the composer we the composition; but so that we might be one thing with him in him, he was willing to be our head by taking flesh from us, in which he could die for us—so to convince you that this whole is the one Christ, he said through Isaiah: *He wound a turban on my head as a bridegroom, he clothed me with ornaments as a bride* (Is 61:10). He's the bridegroom, he's the bride; bridegroom, clearly, in the head, bride in the body. For, says he, *they shall be two in one flesh*, and, *it is no longer two, but one flesh*.[31]

Meconi comments on this sermon text, "[Augustine] is adamant that no created person could ever cross the ontological distinction between God and creation so as to become divine the way Christ is divine."[32] Therefore, totus Christus does not violate the creator/created distinction.

Does the Church Become Infallible or, Worse, Does Jesus Christ Become Fallible?

Since the church and Christ are a united body, does the church now take on the essential sinlessness or the infallible authority of Jesus Christ? Does Christ annex our sin as a part of his essential personhood, or does he lose the independent freedom of his own authoritative infallibility?

30. Augustine, *Expositions of the Psalms* 30.2.4.

31. Augustine, *Sermons* 91.8 (italics original).

32. Meconi, *One Christ*, 212. For more on totus Christus worries in general, see 195–216, and for specific limitations of totus Christus language, see 210–16.

As stated above, Jesus Christ retains his independent existence. This would include his sinlessness and infallibility. Christ makes his church holy but does not make it sinless. Augustine clearly distinguished between the one who saves from sin and the ones who need to be saved: "Let us hear them as one single organism, but let us listen to the Head as Head, and the body as body. The persons are not separated, but in dignity they are distinct, for the Head saves and the body is saved. May the Head dispense mercy, and the body bemoan its misery. The role of the Head is to purge away sins, the body's to confess them."[33]

Burns states succinctly Augustine's perspective: "The sinless head . . . voluntarily shared the mortality and suffering of his members, but the members did not share all the perfections of their divine head: he was creator and mediator; they were not."[34] Jesus Christ does not link his character to the church in a way that would compromise his own righteousness.

Further, Jesus does not deposit his truth in the church in a manner that risks his own independent, absolute authority. Totus Christus does not underwrite elevating church tradition to the level of Jesus Christ's exclusive authority, nor does it necessarily compromise the Protestant doctrine of *sola scriptura*. Granted, some have taken it there.[35] But with a theologically disciplined approach, totus Christus does not, in and of itself, inevitably lead to investing the church—that is, the body of Christ—with infallible authority.

Does Totus Christus Undermine Solus Christus?

Does totus Christus require the church's acts of service and sacrifice to accrue additional merit for justification? Or does the whole-Christ teaching mean that one particular denomination's sacraments are necessary for grace? Does totus Christus necessitate a certain visible church structure be the primary source of grace?

Jesus Christ's salvific work was finished on the cross. He is the one and only and once-and-for-all sacrifice for our sins. No further merit is accrued through the works of Christ in his ecclesial body. In these works, the church experiences the benefits of the salvation they have received in Jesus Christ. Totus Christus does not have to result in a doctrine that implies that Jesus Christ's atoning work is somehow incomplete without the church. When Paul wrote that he fulfills what is lacking in the sufferings of Jesus Christ (Col. 1:24), he

33. Augustine, *Expositions of the Psalms* 30.6.

34. Burns, *Augustine's Preached Theology*, 260.

35. Vanhoozer warns of the dangers of the totus Christus overreach in Roman Catholic ecclesiology in *Biblical Authority After Babel*, 151–53.

means that through his own suffering he fulfills the mission of bringing the message of Jesus Christ's redemptive work—the forgiveness of sins—to the world (Col. 1:14, 24–29). Again, recall that the head saves; the body is saved.

Further, Christ's afflictions and the church's sufferings are shared but distinct. Augustine explains that "Christ is still suffering; but Christ cannot suffer in his own flesh, now glorified in heaven. Christ therefore suffers in my flesh, as it still struggles on earth."[36] Inversely, we fellowship or participate in the sufferings of Christ, but his sufferings in his own flesh are his own. We do not continue the sufferings of Christ as a means of atonement or adding to his merit, but we participate in his sufferings to know Christ in deep intimacy (Phil. 3:7–11).

Due to the present realities on the ecclesiological ground, an emphasis on the autonomy and freedom of Jesus Christ to work through various structures and forms has become necessary. Much has happened in the church since Augustine's day, including the development of Roman Catholic ecclesiology and divisions precipitated by the Protestant Reformation. Christians living after the Reformation view catholicity and unity differently than Augustine could have. Nowadays there are many diverse structures, including differing conceptions of church government, baptism, and the Lord's Supper. Structural and material unity exist as a distant memory and a far-off hope. A retrieval of Augustine's totus Christus does not require one to hold that Jesus Christ, the mediator, gave over the independent power of his own free agency to the baptismal or eucharistic acts or the hierarchical structure of any church or denomination.

The present reality is that the vast majority of Protestant Christians will not accept the Roman Catholic Church's invitation to come home. But all is not bleak. There is ecumenical hope. We can join now in Augustine's vision of the home we are all traveling toward.

With Augustine, we can continue to believe—even though the contemporary church has very different views regarding polity and the sacraments—that the Holy Spirit, as an act of grace, works through baptism and the Lord's Supper to unite the body of Christ and produce within us deep Christian charity, even if the full realization of one baptism and one body (structurally, materially, and functionally) are yet to be. Today, we the church are more like a mosaic—one that is on a transformational pilgrimage, asking, seeking, knocking, receiving, and finding.[37] Jesus Christ is free to work within and without the structures as he sees fit without undermining the value of totus Christus.

36. Augustine, *Expositions of the Psalms* 142.3.
37. Augustine, *Confessions* 13.37.52.

Is Totus Christus an Over-Realized Eschatology?

Does totus Christus get ahead of itself? Does it bring into the present age too much of the deep intimacy that will be experienced between the church and its Savior in the ultimate redemption of all things?

Augustine would not have seen it that way. He conceived of the church as on a pilgrimage—imperfect and suffering—until its unity with Christ is fully realized, when its journey reaches the homeland. Until then, the church will suffer. Commenting on the church's suffering in Psalm 86, Augustine declares, "These tribulations are never lacking to the Church while it makes its pilgrim way through this world; now they afflict some members, now others, for the calamities strike from every direction. This is why the Church says, *All day long*, suggesting the long stretch of time until the world ends."[38] Over time, the church may have developed totus Christus along more triumphalist and over-realized lines, but Augustine's whole-Christ teaching fits within his pilgrim ecclesiology of an imperfect and suffering church on a journey homeward.[39]

Conclusion

True, some have voiced concerns over the implications of Augustine's totus Christus teaching, but the benefits of the doctrine seem to me to far outweigh the potential negatives. What's more, some of the worries appear unfounded, especially when we take a closer look at how Augustine explained and applied the whole Christ to his congregation.

If the whole-Christ teaching seems to you worth retrieving for the purpose of uniting a suffering and fragmented church, then you may wonder, How do pastors help their congregations become conscious of the whole-Christ reality? Or even more importantly, How does the whole Christ become, in practical terms, a means for unity and solidarity in the church? In the next chapter, we look at how to implement the unifying and healing power of the whole-Christ teaching in a congregation through praying the Psalms.

38. Augustine, *Expositions of the Psalms* 87.15 (italics original).

39. See Augustine, *City of God* 19.17. We will discuss Augustine's pilgrim ecclesiology more in chap. 7.

TWO

Praying the Psalms

The *human* Jesus Christ . . . is praying in the Psalter through the mouth of his congregation. The Psalter is the prayer book of Jesus Christ in the truest sense of the word. He prayed the Psalter, and now it has become his prayer for all time.

—Dietrich Bonhoeffer, *Life Together*

The constantly changing patterns of Christ's presence in the Church, and of the Church's in Christ, allowed the expositor to understand all the words of the psalms in equal measure as the prayer of Christ in his totality.

—Maria Boulding, introduction to Augustine's *Expositions of the Psalms*

For no matter what you seek, whether it be repentance and confession, or help in trouble and temptation or under persecution, whether you have been set free from plots and snares or, on the contrary, are sad for any reason, or whether, seeing yourself progressing and your enemy cast down, you want to praise and thank and bless the Lord, each of these things the Divine Psalms show you how to do, and in every case the words you want are written down for you, and you can say them as your own.

—Athanasius, *Letter to Marcellinus*

"Dr. Allen is a mystic."

My son, Colton, let me know that some of my beloved students were discussing my mystic inclinations. They asserted, "Dr. Allen isn't just an academic; he's a mystic." They spoke positively about the mystical aspect that I bring to my teaching and mentoring.

I did not ask them what they meant by "mystic," but I felt a sense of satisfaction that they perceived me that way, because I do desire to know God in a deeply personal way that reaches beyond mere academic knowledge.[1]

My mystic quest started in earnest when I was a young pastor. I was not in the ministry long before I realized that my personal spiritual life was too thin for a vibrant pastoral ministry, so I began to search for resources that would help me develop a deeper—a mystical—experience with God. I discovered a whole world of Christian resources for spiritual contemplation and growth. I began to learn from the writings of Henri Nouwen, Thomas Merton, François Fénelon, Richard Foster, Dallas Willard, Eugene Peterson, and many others. At one point, I completed a doctor of ministry degree at Gordon-Conwell, half of which focused on spiritual renewal movements in church history. Church historian and renewal scholar Richard Lovelace taught the spiritual renewal part of the degree.[2] He entered Yale as an atheist and was converted to Christianity in large part by reading Thomas Merton's *The Seven Storey Mountain*.

In my quest, I was especially attracted to solitude, silence, contemplation, and listening. I began to overcome overthinking through calming my mind in silence. My mind quieted as I realized its limits. This spiritual journey felt very solitary, something that happened mostly when I was by myself, fasting from food, reflecting privately on Scripture, meditating in silence, or walking alone in the woods. I knew that church and community were a part of this journey; I had participated in a long-standing prayer meeting that focused on praying the Psalms. But still, I didn't quite get how mystical life occurred with others until I discovered Augustine's totus Christus theology and his teaching on the relationship of the whole Christ to praying the Psalms. I had experienced God's presence in praying the Psalms with others, but I didn't have a way of articulating the breadth and depth of its mystical meaning.

Today, I am beginning to sense that the most profound Christian mystical experiences occur when the church gathers for worship and prayer. Daily I pray the evening and morning prayers from the 2019 Book of Common Prayer, but now, even when I pray alone, I recognize that I am praying with God's church.

1. While I'm slightly uneasy about the use of the term "mystic," I feel more uncomfortable with an overemphasis on the cognitive in the spiritual life. Yes, God has revealed himself in the words of Scripture. We meditate on these words and turn them over in our minds, but he has revealed in the Bible that there is a love we can know that surpasses knowledge. Paul prays that the Ephesians would be strengthened by the Spirit in their inner beings, that they would comprehend something about God that is beyond comprehension, and that they would be filled with the fullness of God (Eph. 3:14–21). That's what I long for. In that biblical sense, I am a mystic.

2. See Lovelace, *Dynamics of Spiritual Life*.

There is something special that happens when the church gathers for worship. When we gather, we have a communal mystical encounter together. Praying the Psalms as the whole Christ gives us an entrance into a communal spiritual life together. Each Sunday morning at the church I pastor, we stand together and read a psalm responsively at the beginning of the worship service. At that point, Christ prays in us, with us, and for us. We blend our individual voices with the one voice of Jesus Christ.

Let me explain the pastoral and ecclesial value of praying the Psalms from a whole-Christ perspective.

Praying the Psalms

Praying the Psalms as the whole Christ can increase unity and solidarity in the church as the Psalms give voice to our common humanity through the mediation of Christ. We pray together our shared expectations and disappointments, our common hopes and fears, and our mutual happiness in friendship and sadness in loneliness. We bring together our praise to God and the confession of our sins. Together we question God's fairness, and we celebrate his justice. With one voice we complain about our unanswered prayer and give thanks for God's provision. In all this, Christ intercedes for us as we read and pray together.

Praying the Psalms as the whole Christ was not an obscure or minor theme in Augustine's pastoral ministry; it was central. What follows demonstrates the importance of praying the Psalms as the totus Christus to Augustine's pastoral ministry.

The Voice of the Whole Christ in the Psalms

For Augustine, the speaker in the Psalms is the whole Christ—head and body, bridegroom and bride, Christ and the church.[3] Quite simply, the Psalms are the prayers of the totus Christus. But this simplicity is not without its

3. Scholars of biblical hermeneutics refer to this as "prosopological exegesis." See Bates, *Hermeneutics of the Apostolic Proclamation*, 183–221. For contemporary scholars of biblical hermeneutics who may have worries about Augustine's method of reading the Psalms as the prayers of the whole Christ, Augustine's approach can be seen as a combination of three claims made by Richard B. Hays: (1) The Psalms were understood by at least some pre-Christian Jewish interpreters to be prayers of the Messiah as he representatively embodied "the fate of the whole people of Israel"; (2) "Paul's use of the Old Testament is characterized by 'ecclesiocentric exegesis'"; and (3) "Paul bears witness to the practice of reading the Psalms with an imagination converted by the death and resurrection of the *Christos*." Hays, "Christ Prays the Psalms," 101–18.

complexity. Sometimes Augustine identifies the voice praying as the head; at other times, he recognizes the voice as that of the body. Yet even as he identifies different voices, he recognizes that these voices can be distinguished but not separated. The one Christ prays in the Psalms. In these prayers a deep solidarity exists between Christ and his church, as Augustine emphasizes in his exposition of Psalm 85:

> When we speak to God in prayer we do not separate the Son from God, and when the body of the Son prays it does not separate its head from itself. The one sole savior of his body is our Lord Jesus Christ, the Son of God, who prays for us, prays in us, and is prayed to by us. He prays for us as our priest, he prays in us as our head, and he is prayed to by us as our God. Accordingly we must recognize our voices in him, and his accents in ourselves. . . . We pray, then, to him, through him and in him; we speak with him and he speaks with us.[4]

The voices may be distinguished without the solidarity being broken. Many voices pray with one voice: Christ's voice in ours, our many voices together in his.

In his exposition of Psalm 30, while emphasizing the church's "transfiguration," "transaction," and our "wonderful exchange" in Christ, Augustine explains that the head and the body speak as one:

> This is the wonderful exchange, the divine business deal, the transaction effected in this world by the heavenly dealer. He came to receive insults and give honors, he came to drain the cup of suffering and give salvation, he came to undergo death and give life. Facing death, then, because of what he had from us, he was afraid, not in himself but in us. When he said that his soul was sorrowful to the point of death, we all unquestionably said it with him. Without him, we are nothing, but in him we too are Christ. Why? Because the whole Christ consists of Head and body. The Head is he who is the savior of his body, he who has already ascended into heaven; but the body is the Church, toiling on earth.[5]

Christ and the church speak with one voice. He speaks in our words so that we can speak in his. Prayers of rest and toil, guilt and innocence, courage and

4. Augustine, *Expositions of the Psalms* 85.1, quoted in Meconi, *One Christ*, 207.

5. Augustine, *Expositions of the Psalms* 30.2.3. Here, in his exposition of Psalm 30, he refers to his favorite "whole-Christ" text, Acts 9:4, demonstrating that while Christ was seated in heaven he could not have been suffering Saul's persecutions, yet he confronted Paul for inflicting injuries against him. How could Christ say this? "The Head was crying out on behalf of the members, and the Head was transfiguring the members into himself." The whole Christ spoke with one anguished voice. The same is true in the Psalms.

fear, shame and honor, delight and frustration, defeat and triumph, praise and lament unite in a singular cry to God. Holy solidarity.

Yet within the one voice, two speakers can be distinguished. Turning to Matthew 19:5–6, Ephesians 5:31–32, and Isaiah 61:10, Augustine demonstrates how two—the bridegroom and the bride—become one flesh. Then he asks, "If two in one flesh, why not two in one voice?" Then he applies this to the two voices of Christ and the church, which are considered one voice in their prayers: "Let Christ speak, then, because in Christ the Church speaks, and in the Church Christ speaks, and the body speaks in the Head, and the Head in the body."[6]

In Augustine's exposition of Psalm 56, he speaks a beautiful word about Christ's personal solidarity in our suffering: "He [Christ] would not have us speaking apart from him, any more than he wants to be apart from us, for he said, *Lo, I am with you even to the end of the ages* (Mt 28:20). If he is with us, he speaks in us, speaks about our concerns, and speaks through us, because we also speak in him; and only because we speak in him do we speak the truth."[7] In his exposition of Psalm 62, he says it very plainly: "His voice is our voice too, and our voice his."[8]

To clarify, the prayers that the church prays with Christ in the Psalms are not just the prayers of an individual (though certainly each of us can pray them from the depths of our personal sufferings, longings, and sins), and they are not simply the prayers of a single local church (though truly a local gathering of believers prays these prayers from their unique joys, sufferings, and confessions in a certain time and place), but these are the prayers of the universal church for all times in all places.

Michael Cameron explains how the different voices speak as one voice: "Different voices might speak (Christ, Church, Christian), though each speaks within what Augustine called the *totus*, 'the whole.' The consonance of interpretations stressed the conjunction of voices; the individual Christian prays *within* the Church's voice, just as the Church prays *within* the voice of Christ. The different voices of the body and the head speak in unison (*simul*) with Christ's voice, but the Church and its members speak *through him*."[9] Cameron's three categories—Christ, the church, and the Christian—clarify both the distinctions and the interrelatedness of all the voices in Christ's one voice. The distinctions and connections are realized as we pray the Psalms, the distinct accents recognized in the one voice.

6. Augustine, *Expositions of the Psalms* 30.2.4.
7. Augustine, *Expositions of the Psalms* 56.1 (italics original).
8. Augustine, *Expositions of the Psalms* 62.2.
9. Cameron, *Christ Meets Me Everywhere*, 183–84 (italics original).

Thus, we as individuals and as local churches pray these prayers in solidarity with all members of the body in all times and in every place: "Now the whole Christ consists of head and body. . . . His body is the Church: not this or that local church, but the Church that extends throughout the world. It is made up not only of people alive today, for those who have gone before us belong to the Church too, and so do those who will come after us, even to the end of time."[10]

Yet each of us may hear our own voice in Christ's voice. As a part of Christ's body, we hear his voice in our individual voice and ours in his: "This is how we should hear Christ speaking. Yet each one of us should at the same time hear his or her own voice, since we are all organically parts of Christ's body. Sometimes he will speak words that none of us can recognize as our own, for they belong only to the head, but even then Christ does not divorce himself from our words and withdraw into his own, nor does he go so far away as not to return from his own words to ours."[11]

Whether leading my congregation in a responsive reading of a psalm or praying a psalm aloud in my private prayer time, I try to remain conscious of Jesus Christ praying for me, with me, and in me. But more than that, my voice joins with my local church and, beyond that, the universal church. Using our praying imaginations, together we become aware of the head and the body, praying our joys and sorrows and our laments and praises with one voice. In these prayers, we experience Christ's mediation uniting our hearts and bringing us hope and healing.

Sin and Holiness: Praying the Psalms with the Whole Christ

Augustine recognized a significant issue that his congregation could raise related to praying the Psalms as the whole Christ. How can the voice of Christ be represented when the psalmist confesses sin? How can the voice of the church be represented when the psalmist declares his own holiness? Christ does not sin; the church does. Christ is holy; the church isn't. Augustine does more than simply solve the dilemma; he turns this problem into an occasion for instructing congregants in their Christian walk.

In his exposition of Psalm 140, Augustine clarifies that when the psalmist speaks of "the tale of my sins," Christ speaks about his ecclesial body, not himself. Christ's sinless voice speaks in solidarity with our sinful voice. Augustine uses this as an opportunity to humble his hearers and instruct them to confess their sins: "But if this is so, can anyone among [Christ's] members

10. Augustine, *Expositions of the Psalms* 56.1.
11. Augustine, *Expositions of the Psalms* 140.3.

pretend to have no sin? Only someone who is so bold as to flaunt himself and claim a spurious holiness and accuse Christ of falsehood. Confess, then, you who are a member of Christ, that your head spoke there for you."[12]

Can this work in the opposite direction? What if the psalmist claims to be holy? Does that mean that the church is inherently holy? When Christ speaks of his own holiness in the Psalms, does the church make the same claim about itself? Again, Augustine uses this dilemma as an opportunity for instruction. Commenting on the psalmist's claim "I am holy," Augustine explains that this is not the body's own inherent holiness but the holiness it receives from the head:

> It is his voice, then, that I recognize when I hear the words, *I am holy*, but must I exclude mine from his? No; I can be certain that when he speaks, he speaks inseparably from his body. Shall even I then dare to say, *I am holy*? If I meant "holy" in the sense of making others holy and standing in no need of anyone to sanctify me, I should be arrogant to claim it, and a liar; but if it means "holy" in the sense of "made holy," as scripture uses the phrase, *Be holy, because I am holy* ([Lev.] 19:2), then yes, let Christ's body dare to say it, let this one single person who cries from the ends of the earth dare to say with his head and in subordination to his head, *I am holy*, for he has received the grace of holiness, the grace of baptism and the forgiveness of sins.[13]

In the same paragraph he will warn that if they claim to be holy only by their own efforts, they are proud, but to say that as faithful members of the body they are not holy is an act of ingratitude. Worse, if they cast doubt on the holiness of members of the body, they insult Christ, their head.

The members of the body can confess with their head in one voice, "I am a sinner" (though their sin is theirs alone), and claim, "I am holy" (though their holiness is Christ's). Yet within the one Christ, there exists deep solidarity between the head and the body. Two accents in one voice. Two voices in one prayer.

The Pastoral Benefits of Praying the Psalms This Way

Augustine's theology cannot be abstracted from his pastoral ministry. Augustine shepherded his flock through the exposition of Scripture, and from this expositional ministry emerged his totus Christus teaching. For Augustine, the Psalms provide a way for his congregation—and ours today—to experience together the solidarity of the whole Christ as it voices our united pain and

12. Augustine, *Expositions of the Psalms* 140.6.
13. Augustine, *Expositions of the Psalms* 85.4.

fears. Rowan Williams acknowledges Augustine's pastoral goal of helping the congregation recognize as their own the frustrations and the fears expressed in the Psalms: "[Augustine's] aim is not to elaborate a theology in a vacuum, but to enable believers to make the text of the Psalm their own, to speak it out of their own concerns and anxieties. And central to this is the recognition that Christ has first made these words *his* own. . . . The point is that the *pastoral* goal of the sermon is inseparable from the clear theological principle of our incorporation into Christ and Christ's assuming of our human voice."[14] Our sufferings and sins are taken up by Christ as his own. We pray them as our human experience finds voice in the voice of Jesus Christ.

What follows expands on the pastoral gains of praying the Psalms as the whole Christ. These are some of the benefits of reading and praying the Psalms this way.

1. We Experience the Wonderful Exchange

Whether they truly realize it or not, Christians sitting in a church five minutes before the worship service have experienced a "wonderful exchange." Christ has transposed himself into them. As a result, their ability to read the Psalms has changed even if they are not fully aware of it. They now "read through the eyes of the one who fulfilled Scripture by transposing himself into his members."[15]

Christ has transposed himself into us, and he has also transfigured us into himself. He is in us, and we are in him. As the whole Christ, he is us, and we are him. Reading the Psalms as the whole Christ enables us to bring this exchange into the reality of our worship and thus into the experience of our everyday lives. "The word that Augustine eventually selects to elucidate the spiritual exchange is *transfigurare*: 'to transfigure.'"[16] Augustine often uses this term to explain a totus Christus reading of the Psalms—for example, "But in fact he who deigned to assume the form of a slave, and within that form to clothe us with himself, he who did not disdain to take us up into himself, did not disdain either to transfigure us into himself [*transfigurare in se*], and to speak in our words, so that we in our turn might speak in his."[17] In *Confessions*, Augustine employs this word to demonstrate that in humility Christ Jesus used his own human flesh to "make a bridge to bring [pretentious selves] to himself."[18]

14. Williams, *On Augustine*, 38–39 (italics original).
15. Cameron, *Christ Meets Me Everywhere*, 289.
16. Cameron, *Christ Meets Me Everywhere*, 290.
17. Augustine, *Expositions of the Psalms* 30.2.3.
18. Augustine, *Confessions* 7.18.24.

Confessions may be thought of as Augustine's account of the lived experience of the transfigured life, the life that Augustine prays in the Psalms. Thus, his life becomes, as recorded in *Confessions*, the working of a life formed by praying the Psalms. The exchanged life is entered experientially and practically, at least in part, through praying the Psalms. Jason Byassee, commenting on Augustine's consistent christological exegesis of the Psalms, makes this point: "Christ speaks . . . *representationally*, so that later readers and followers will notice themselves in the story and will pray and confess accordingly. And . . . Christ speaks . . . *transfiguratively*, so that those who speak these words and imitate these actions will themselves be changed into Christ."[19] Through praying the Psalms together as the whole Christ, we will enter and inhabit our own "confessions" story—even as we live out and in our own Psalms story.

Let's take the example of the fear of death to illustrate this point. If they are honest with themselves, everyone in that sanctuary fears death. Some fear the prospect of a slow death or the possible pain of death. Others worry about going to hell. Some are haunted by the sense of losing control at death. Even those with a strong assurance of salvation are sometimes bothered by a niggle of doubt. The fear of death is a kind of death itself. Yet Christ has transposed himself into our troubling fear and dreadful sorrow. We see this when he invokes Psalm 42:5 in Gethsemane: "My soul is overwhelmed with sorrow to the point of death" (Matt. 26:38 NIV). Cameron comments on this verse, "[Jesus] speaks out of every human being's mortal fear."[20]

When these fearful church members join their voices in the voice of Jesus Christ and pray this psalm together, they experience the wonderful exchange. Jesus enters our fears and brings them to the Father. Death is still real, but in Christ we discover healing for our sorrowful souls and the hope for our death-bound bodies. Jesus was alone in this fear—even though it was our fear and not his own—so we do not have to be. A wonderful exchange has taken place—he experienced our fear and sorrow so that we could receive his hope and healing—and we can enter the experienced reality of it through praying the Psalms.

2. We Are Transformed

The astounding exchange catalyzes our transformation. A totus Christus praying of the Psalms is more than a mere devotional, informational, or instructional reading of the Psalms; rather, "it unseals deep places, emotions

19. Byassee, *Praise Seeking Understanding*, 75 (italics original).
20. Cameron, *Christ Meets Me Everywhere*, 290.

otherwise buried, and it provides an analogy for the unity or intelligibility of a human life lived in faith. Here is a conversation with God that has a beginning, a middle and an end. And in the course of that conversation, the human speaker is radically changed and enabled to express what is otherwise hidden from him or her: Augustine speaks of what the Psalm he is discussing (Psalm 4, *Cum invocarem*) 'makes of him': the act of recitation becomes an opening to the transforming action of grace ([*Confessions*] IX.4.8)."[21] Through praying the Psalms, we are rescripted, drawn up into Christ's story.

But this is not just a cognitive worldview story that we assent to and align with—one that we could write up in a college-freshman Christian-worldview paper. Nor is it merely a biblical narrative script that we must improvise because we live somewhere between the ascension of Christ and his second coming.[22] It is that, but more. A whole-life way of praying the Psalms transfigures our lives into a living worldview and brings the script alive because we are in Christ and Christ is in us. We are equipped to—in the words of my friend Josh Chatraw—"tell a better story" because we are being formed organically in Christ's better story.[23] Through praying the Psalms, we begin to learn the dynamics of what that means—our lives are re-storied according to the Psalms.

As stated above, Augustine models this for us in *Confessions*, first by beginning the book with a quote from the Psalms and then drawing on the Psalms throughout *Confessions*.[24] Michael Cameron notes the phenomenon: "This [totus Christus] mode of reading [the Psalms] shapes the pattern of Scripture quotations that quilts the *Confessions*. Augustine does not merely use Scripture for 'support,' but *speaks from within Scripture as if its words are his own words*."[25] Augustine invites his audience to pray the Psalms because the Psalter welcomes its readers into the very life of the biblical narrative, whose central actor and action is Jesus Christ. In the life of Christ, the church—and we as individual parts of the body—embodies the narrative. The Psalms, prayed in a whole-Christ way, are an entrance into the life of the biblical story and stories. The church is really and substantially re-storied—transformed inside and out.

Imagine for a moment if the genre of each parishioner's story were floating above their heads as they sat in anticipation of the service: "fantasy,"

21. Williams, *On Augustine*, 26.

22. See Wells, *Improvisation*, 45–70; Vanhoozer, *Drama of Doctrine*, 2–3, 335–44.

23. See the section "More than a Strategy" in Chatraw, *Telling a Better Story*, 224.

24. As Sarah Ruden notes on the first page of her translation, "As throughout the *Confessions*, Augustine draws phrases from the Psalms; here he echoes Psalms 48:1, 96:4, 145:3, and 147:5." Augustine, *Confessions: A New Translation*, 3.

25. Cameron, *Christ Meets Me Everywhere*, 289 (italics original).

"tragedy," "action and adventure," "romance," "dystopian," "horror," "historical fiction," "mystery," or perhaps the scariest of them all, "short story." What if those stories could be reimagined and rewritten with a different direction and a better ending? This direction and ending could be cultivated through a sustained weekly rescripting of their lives by a totus Christus reading of the Psalms. Floating above their heads would be "Christ," each time written with a different script but united in one hopeful, beautiful story. Praying the Psalms opens the church up to this transforming grace.

3. We Find Ourselves, Our Common Humanity, and Our Life in Christ

Praying the Psalms as the whole Christ, the congregation gives voice to its common humanity and comes to see itself in the mirror of the Psalms. In his exposition of Psalm 45, Augustine instructs the congregation to cling to one another to recognize themselves in this psalm: "So let us recognize ourselves here, and see whether the following lines in the main text of the psalm fit our situation. We shall find ourselves in them as long as we remain inseparably united to the members of that body whose Head is in heaven."[26] Being united to Jesus Christ, the congregation, in its very own time-and-space situation, finds itself in the Psalms.

Cameron elucidates this exposition of Psalm 45 with another text from Augustine's *Expositions of the Psalms*: "Scripture reflects the Church to itself: 'Everything written here is our mirror' (*Exp. 2 Ps.* 30.3.1). . . . 'If the psalm prays, then you pray; if it grieves, then you grieve; if it exults, then you rejoice; if it hopes, then you hope; and if it fears, then you fear' (ibid.). The head figuratively urges his members to find themselves in Scripture, for the Church knows its identity only there." Cameron continues, "Its members not only read the Bible's words as words about Christ the head: *they live as Christ inside these words and so speak them as their own words*. They own, understand, and speak Scripture with the warmth of Christ's own self-understanding."[27] J. Patout Burns Jr. adds, "The mystery of their lives and deaths were being enacted, displayed, and revealed in his. They were being called to recognize themselves in him: to feel the same fear and pain, to exercise the same trust in the Father."[28] The church and its members are to see their voices joined with Christ's voice in the voice of Scripture.

In his exposition of Psalm 143, Augustine encourages his congregation to hear the words of the psalm as their own: "You must therefore not assume

26. Augustine, *Expositions of the Psalms* 45.1.
27. Cameron, *Christ Meets Me Everywhere*, 289 (italics original).
28. Burns, *Augustine's Preached Theology*, 276–77.

that anything you hear spoken in reference to Christ himself is no concern of yours. It does concern you, because you are members of Christ."[29] Rowan Williams comments, "The church as a whole is revealed as the community where humanity is allowed full scope to say what it is, in terms of its failure and pain, so that it may fully become what it is created to be."[30] In its praying of the Psalms, the congregation expresses together what it is: a suffering and sinful people being saved through the mediation of Christ. Williams connects the church's praying the Psalms as the whole Christ with its salvation: "The meaning of our salvation is that we are included in his life, given the right to speak with his divine voice, reassured that what our human voices say out of darkness and suffering has been owned by him as his voice, so that it may in some way be opened to the life of God for healing or forgiveness."[31]

One middle-aged man sits in the congregation distraught over a broken marriage; a young man bows his head, riddled with guilt over another moral failure; an abused wife struggles to find any sense of agency. They join their voices to pray the words of the psalm and the words of their Savior: "My God, my God, why have you forsaken me?" (Ps. 22:1 NIV). The whole Christ prays with them and for them. They are not nobody. They are not alone. They do not suffer in silence. Christ takes up their pain within himself and gives voice to their angst. In their united prayer, they are experiencing the *fellowship* of Christ's suffering (Phil. 3:10–11). The dead are made alive with the resurrection life of Christ. Praying the Psalms this way is truly "an appropriation of Christ's life, in history and eternity."[32] The pastor doesn't have to comfort all those who suffer, because the whole Christ already does that for them.

In reading and praying the Psalms this way, we discover who we are, connect with one another in our common broken humanity, and experience the life of Christ within and among us. A fractured church finds solidarity in reading together these psalms. We join our voices in one voice, praying with him, through him, and to him as he prays in us and for us.

4. We Are United in Christ

With his characteristic eloquence, Augustine asserts, in his exposition of Psalm 147, the unity Christians have in the whole Christ: "Because there are many of us, we praise him all together, and because we are one, we praise him as one. The many are the same as the one, because he in whom we are

29. Augustine, *Expositions of the Psalms* 143.1.
30. Williams, *On Augustine*, 30.
31. Williams, *On Augustine*, 29.
32. Williams, *On Augustine*, 30.

one is himself always one, undivided."[33] No matter how divided by cultural currents, doctrinal peculiarities, or sinful tendencies, the disparate members of the congregation are united in the prayers of Christ. Christian unity and a totus Christus approach to the Psalms were deeply related for Augustine. David Vincent Meconi writes, "Prayer and praise are never isolated moments but originate from Christ's humble identification with his faithful. . . . Like charity, prayer can never be divided amongst individual worshippers but is assured a co-inherence by the concord between Christ and Christians."[34]

Our individual voices find co-inherence in the communal voice as we pray the Psalms together. This communal praying enables us to read our unique anxieties and complaints from the same script. Rowan Williams makes this point: "Scripture defines the character of a life in conversation and communion with God; and it is most fruitful for the believer when it provides a 'script' for such a conversation." But this is not a lifeless reciting of a text; instead, our reading is inhabited and united by Christ's own life-giving action. Williams continues, "First and foremost, however, we must recognize that the essence of Christ's own action in the incarnation is a matter of 'transfiguring' the human voice, which, in turn, is essentially a matter of defining a *communal* voice that is nonetheless the only medium for the personal voice."[35] We are united in the one voice. Again, his life is transposed into ours, and our voice is transfigured into his. In this, many voices are made one and united through one script: the Psalms.

The smiling welcomers, the cloistered family, and the uncomfortable loners all pray from a singular script, united by the same Holy Spirit in the one voice of Christ. Each has come from a unique place and traveled a different path to get there. Their fears, disappointments, and hopes are not the same, but they are shared as the congregation prays the Psalms as the whole Christ. Many pray-ers united in the one pray-er.

5. Christ Intercedes for Us and We for One Another

From Scripture we know that Christ is our mediator and that he intercedes for us (Rom. 8:34; 1 Tim. 2:5; Heb. 7:25; 1 John 2:1). In coming down to us, he entered our world (John 16:28; 1 Tim. 1:15). As Christ died for us and rose from the dead, we died with him and were raised from the dead (Rom. 6:4; Eph. 2:6; Col. 2:12). He is our mediator who brings us to God. As such, he intercedes for us. We know that. But praying the Psalms with a whole-Christ

33. Augustine, *Expositions of the Psalms* 147.7.
34. Meconi, *One Christ*, 207–8.
35. Williams, *On Augustine*, 34 (italics original).

perspective actualizes this truth for us. His voice is our voice, and our voice is his voice.

Commenting on the words of the crucified Christ in Psalm 21, "*The tale of my sins leaves me far from salvation*," Augustine asks, "What sins could these be, when it was said of Christ, *He committed no sin, nor was any guile found on his lips* (1 Pt 2:22)? How, then, could he say, *the tale of my sins*, except because he himself intercedes for our sins, and has made our sins his own, in order to make his righteousness ours?"[36]

Again, in the anguished question "My God, my God, why have you forsaken me?" we are assured of the compassion of God. "The outcome [of whole-life praying of the Psalms] is a pedagogy of pastoral compassion, partially offered here. In the state of spiritual darkness, we are tempted to think that God is absent, yet when we hear Christ speaking 'our' words of anguish, we know that this cannot be so."[37] Christ is interceding for us as we pray the Psalms, giving voice to our anguish.

Commenting on the same anguished prayer (coming from the lips of the psalmist, Christ, and the church!), Byassee refers to this as "*representational Christology*—in which Christ represents humanity before God, and divinity before humans. That word, 'representational,' or perhaps more strongly and biblically, 'mediatorial,' should be taken to include all these dramatic, corporal, and priestly connotations."[38] Jesus Christ mediates God to us and us to God. He intercedes for us as we pray the Psalms together.

To add another layer of pastoral compassion, we are reminded by Burns that Christ shares his intercessory role with the church. We participate in it as we join our voices in reading the Psalms:

> As head, Christ shared that intercessory role with his body, the church, whose members prayed for one another under his headship. The priestly status of the clergy, [Augustine] argued, derived from that of Christ . . . through the faithful who formed the body of the Whole Christ, the church that elected the clergy to serve it as overseers and governors. . . . Augustine consistently eliminated the privileged role of the clergy as mediators between God and the people. . . . The mediating role belonged to Christ. The full body of the faithful was endowed with the powers and charged with the mission of its Savior, head, and bridegroom. The role proper to the church's officers was oversight and maintaining order.[39]

36. Augustine, *Expositions of the Psalms* 21.2.3 (italics original).
37. Williams, *On Augustine*, 28.
38. Byassee, *Praise Seeking Understanding*, 73 (italics original).
39. Burns, *Augustine's Preached Theology*, 266, 279.

"I'll pray for you." We say this all the time. Perhaps several in the congregation said this just before the worship service. If on that morning the church prays the Psalms together, then they will fulfill their commitment. The head and the body are united in intercessory prayer, representing the specific needs of everyone as they articulate together the prayers, laments, and confessions of the Psalms.

Primarily, Christ shepherds the church, and the church shepherds one another in Christ. The whole Christ is the better pastor. The head intercedes on behalf of the body, and the body, together with its head, intercedes for the body. Our particularized prayers voiced through the generalized words of the Psalms participate specifically in Christ's intercession on our behalf and more broadly in our prayers for one another.

We sometimes imagine Christ interceding for us, but when we read the Psalms together as the whole Christ, we do not have to imagine it. Christ is mediating our concerns to God as we intercede for one another.

6. Christ Suffers with Us and We with Him

We have all heard the statement "There are no words." Oftentimes when we say this, we are hurting so badly that we can't put it in words; we feel numb and voiceless. In the Psalms, Jesus Christ gives words to our pain, loneliness, disappointments, losses, and frustrations. But to pray the Psalms with the whole Christ is not just to recite comforting words but to enter, through charity and the Holy Spirit, into deep solidarity with Jesus Christ. He gives voice to our sufferings. The pain of the universal church in all times and all places, the disappointments of the local church, and the loneliness of the individual Christian—all interrelated—are taken up into the cries of the voice of the Messiah in us, with us, through us, and for us. Jesus speaks in the voice of his suffering church.[40]

In a letter to Senator Mark Hatfield dated April 8, 1986, Henri Nouwen, the author of the spiritual classic *The Wounded Healer*, shares pastoral reflections on the body of Christ's suffering with its crucified head. First, Nouwen focuses on the cross of Jesus Christ, identifying Jesus as "God-with-us," the sinless one who took on all of humanity's pain and offered himself as a worthy sacrifice to the Father. Then, Nouwen shares from his own observations how the body of Christ's suffering bears witness to the crucified Christ:

> I am always struck that poor people are so attracted to images of the suffering Christ. In Spain and Latin America Good Friday often seems even more important

40. Williams, *On Augustine*, 29.

> than Easter. There is a certain realism here. People are looking for strength to live their hard life faithfully. They often find more consolation in knowing that God is with them in the struggle, in the agony and even in the experience of being abandoned by God, than in the knowledge that finally life will prove stronger than death. For most people the most burning question is: how to make it another day, another week, another year. Looking at the crucified Jesus in his desolation they can say: "But we are not alone, he is with us." There we come to understand fully what it means that God is compassionate, that God is a God who suffers with us.

Nouwen continues,

> Here is revealed to us the deepest meaning of history: it is the full unfolding of the immense suffering that God has suffered on the cross in Jesus Christ. This also is the full unfolding of God's unfathomable love for us. Here also you can catch a glimpse of the mystery of the Church as the body of Christ. What we see happening in Nicaragua, Guatemala, El Salvador, Ireland, South Africa, Iran and Iraq is much more than a series of political tragedies that cause much human suffering. It is the manifestation of the immensity of God's pain for our sake. It is a "new" way revealing how much Jesus suffered on the cross. In his humanity we see the body suffering. I often see with my eyes of faith the body of Christ stretched out over our Globe crying out "God, my God, why have you forsaken us." What moves me most is that this vision fills me as much with hope as with anguish.[41]

Williams assures us, "The Psalm text is always the whole Church speaking in the voice of its Head who takes to himself all the experiences and sufferings of the Body."[42] Further, the suffering voice of Psalm 22 becomes paradigmatic, for our head speaks in, with, and for the body: "Obviously, the opening of Psalm 22 (21 in the Lxx used by Augustine) is central, and Augustine reverts to it many times: 'My God, my God, why have you forsaken me?' is a kind of paradigm of how Christ as Head speaks for the Body."[43] Yet Williams expands on the benefits of sharing in the sufferings of Christ: "The Head-and-Body theology thus provides not only a pastoral understanding of what any believer suffers, but an interpretation of it as creatively building up the outworking of Christ's saving act in contingent history. It is not only that Christ accompanies the sufferer, sharing his or her pain; the sufferer is drawn into the action of Christ that ultimately overcomes all sin and grief."[44]

41. Nouwen, *Love, Henri*, 127–28.
42. Williams, *On Augustine*, 38.
43. Williams, *On Augustine*, 28.
44. Williams, *On Augustine*, 29.

There is not a single sufferer in the congregation that morning—the abused, the marginalized, the anxious, the guilty, the shamed, the disappointed, the lonely, the fearful—with whom, in whom, and for whom the whole Christ does not suffer. And in their suffering, they are being brought into the saving action of Christ as he ultimately overcomes the world's sin and grief.

Conclusion

The whole Christ is a better pastor. The totus Christus can bear the heavy weight of the pastoral ministry of the church. Praying the Psalms as the whole Christ provides an entrance into a whole-Christ way of doing pastoral ministry. But that pastor standing in the back of the sanctuary on that Sunday morning must remind the congregation and himself regularly of these truths. Of course, praying the Psalms as the whole Christ is not a panacea for all church ills, but it is a way to shift the focus of pastoral ministry from a single, mere human to the totus Christus. Augustine realized the power of the teaching and frequently reminds his congregation of this way of reading the Psalms. After speaking directly to his congregation about the whole Christ speaking in the Psalms, he reminds them of the prevalence of this truth in Scripture and the profitability of him repeating this teaching:

> These things are not new to you, for you are always hearing them from us. But it is necessary that they be recalled from time to time, partly because the scriptures on which we preach are so closely connected among themselves that many truths recur in many different passages, and partly also because it is profitable for you to hear these things again. Preoccupation with worldly matters can cause thorns to spring up and choke the seed. You need therefore to be reminded by the Lord fairly often of things which the world tries to make you forget.[45]

The church needs a new and better pastor. Not a change of pastors but a changed pastor—one who leads the congregation back to the whole Christ and takes them there again and again. Or better yet, the congregation needs a change of pastors: from the pastor who has come to the end of themself to the whole Christ, from the frazzled head and fatigued body of the one pastor to the united head and body of the whole Christ. The church needs the pastoral ministry of the totus Christus to transform them, unite them, intercede for them, and suffer with them. In the whole Christ, they will find themselves, their common humanity, and their truest life.

The whole Christ is the good shepherd and the better pastor.

45. Augustine, *Expositions of the Psalms* 140.3.

PART TWO

The Whole Person

THREE

Loving Administration

For the foundational principle of the spiritual life is the love of God in Christ poured out upon us through the Holy Spirit. . . . And this principle now flows into all of life, into all the thoughts and deeds of the spiritual person. Love of God gives stature and form to the spiritual life; it organizes and inspires it, turning it into one beautiful organic whole which functions as the foundational *life-force*.

—Herman Bavinck, *Reformed Ethics* (italics original)

In running the church I use language that is descriptive and motivational. I want people to be informed so there are no misunderstandings. And I want people to be motivated so things get done. But in the cure of souls I am far more interested in who people are and who they are becoming in Christ than I am in what they know or what they are doing. In this I soon find that neither descriptive nor motivational language helps very much.

—Eugene Peterson, *The Contemplative Pastor*

He's the real healer; you are only his healing agent.

—Harold Senkbeil, *The Care of Souls*

"Because I have to run this damn church."

This jarring sentence stuck in my pastoral psyche, capturing the way I had often felt about my ministerial responsibilities. It serves as the punch line to a story in Eugene Peterson's memoir, *The Pastor*. Peterson was visiting with a pastor friend named Tom in Baltimore. Peterson recounts the incident that occurred at a diner across from Tom's church:

> Tom and the waitress exchanged greetings. He introduced me to her, "Vanessa." . . . Our coffee mugs were empty. As we were preparing to leave the diner, I went to the washroom. As I returned, Venessa and Tom were engaged in what was obviously an intense conversation. I took a stool at the end of the counter and picked up a newspaper so as not to interrupt them. In a few minutes, Tom joined me and we walked out into the street.
>
> Tom said, "Eugene, did you see us talking, the way *she* was talking—that intensity? I wish I could do that kind of thing all day long, every day. Every time I come in here and there are no customers, she wants to talk about prayer and her life."
>
> "So, why don't you do it—have conversations like that?"
>
> "Because I have to run this damn church."[1]

I know what he is talking about. Perhaps you do as well. But how does pastoring a church become an irritation? How does the place of Christ's rest become a bed of anxiety for his shepherds? How do we keep a hospital for healing from becoming merely a business to run?

In another one of his books, *The Contemplative Pastor: Returning to the Art of Spiritual Direction*, Peterson points at the word "run" as the key to understanding how our church becomes overwhelming because of administrative duties. He tells another story from just before his ordination. It was the first time he had heard the phrase "running a church":

> I was traveling with a pastor I respected very much. I was full of zest and vision, anticipating pastoral life. My inner conviction of call to the pastorate was about to be confirmed by others. What God wanted me to do, what I wanted to do, and what others wanted me to do were about to converge. From fairly extensive reading about pastor and priest predecessors, I was impressed that everyday pastoral life was primarily concerned with developing a life of prayer among the people. Leading worship, preaching the gospel, and teaching Scripture on Sundays would develop in the next six days into representing the life of Christ in the human traffic of the everyday.
>
> With my mind full of these thoughts, my pastor friend and I stopped at a service station for gasoline. My friend, a gregarious person, bantered with the attendant. Something in the exchange provoked a question.
>
> "What do you do?"
>
> "I run a church."
>
> No answer could have surprised me more. I knew, of course, that pastoral life included institutional responsibilities, but it never occurred to me that I

1. Peterson, *The Pastor*, 144–45.

> would be defined by those responsibilities. But the moment I became ordained, I found I was so defined both by the pastors and executives over me and by the parishioners around me.[2]

His description of his first job omitted the pastoral responsibilities of prayer, worship, preaching, and teaching. Shocking, or perhaps not so much. As he puts it, running a church has nothing to do with the ancient practice of the cure of souls—ancient because it goes so far back that it is a tradition that Augustine inherits and develops. It is a primary work of the pastor, one that energizes the pastor and enlivens the church.

This chapter and the next will attempt to rescue the pastor from the debilitating effects of "running" a church and demonstrate how to cure souls through shepherding the congregation in the daily flow of pastoral life and leadership. In doing this, we will not leave Augustine's whole-Christ ecclesiology behind but demonstrate its importance to administration and preaching.

Of course, pastors will always have administrative responsibilities in their daily ministry. But with a focus on curing souls—beginning with word and sacrament—simple tasks and vital leadership moments can become opportunities for spiritual healing, for the church members and for the pastor. Before looking at his therapeutic preaching, we will have to understand Augustine's anthropology, including how he viewed the relationship between believing, understanding, and loving, along with how he saw the relationship between the affections, the will, and the mind.[3] And along the way in this chapter, we will apply his anthropology to the daily pastoral duties, which often include running the church. Before we can administrate and preach in healing and helpful ways, we have to ask ourselves anthropological questions like "What is a human?" "How do we know and decide?" "How do we exercise agency?" "Who are we?"

Faith, Reason, and Love

The people in the orbit of our ministry are primarily lovers—lovers who also believe and think. We fittingly use the term "believers" to refer to Christians,

2. Peterson, *Contemplative Pastor*, 57–58.

3. The word "therapeutic" is used here to describe the process of healing the human experience of being wounded and broken by our own sinfulness and by the fallenness of the world. It is not the same thing as David Brooks's "the Big Me"; Philip Rieff's "born to be pleased"; Christian Smith's "Moralistic Therapeutic Deism"; or Charles Taylor's "therapeutic turn." See Brooks, *Road to Character*, 6–8; C. Smith, *Soul Searching*, 118–71; Rieff, *Triumph of the Therapeutic*; Taylor, *Secular Age*, 618–23.

but perhaps a greater moniker for followers of Jesus Christ would be "lovers." After all, the greatest theological virtue is love (1 Cor. 13:13). In *Teaching Christianity*, Augustine defines love: "What I mean by charity or love is any urge of the spirit to find joy in God for his own sake, and in oneself and one's neighbor for God's sake."[4]

In *The Logic of the Heart: Augustine, Pascal, and the Rationality of Faith*, James R. Peters claims, "Central to Augustine's theory of reason and faith is his conviction that our reasoning about how to live well as humans ought to be directed and molded by our needs and desires as feeling agents who are fundamentally, and above all else, lovers."[5]

Lovers Who Reason

Being lovers affects how we reason and why we use our reason. Peters writes,

> What Augustine refers to . . . as reason is not reason thought of as a mere blind machine, indifferently processing data, but reason as seeking an end and thus as being passionate and desiring. . . . Augustinian reasoning is not a neutral technological process but is an ethical and teleological activity. As Augustine states, reason by its very nature seeks to know and thus possess and enjoy the good. . . . The Augustinian rational person employs reason neither to master nature nor simply to see why things are as they are, but to become the sort of person whose internal order enables him or her, by God's grace, to find his or her proper place in the order of creation.[6]

We are not simply logic choppers. We are lovers who think. We use our thinking to discover what our hearts are searching for. Our rationality is affected by what we want. Trying to lead or persuade folks in the church by mere rational arguments can cause mutual frustration. The truest, most beautiful, and best human loves—God and neighbor—should shape the way we reason with others. This shapes the way we influence them in administrative tasks.

Lovers Who Believe to Understand

But we are getting ahead of ourselves. There's more to administration and persuasion than just viewing people as lovers who think. We must have a framework in which to love and think. This is where belief comes in. Which framework should we believe in, or in which authority should we put our faith

4. Augustine, *Teaching Christianity* 3.10.16.
5. Peters, *Logic of the Heart*, 60.
6. Peters, *Logic of the Heart*, 71.

to best love and think? Which way of conceiving the world makes the most sense for our quest? Which rationality is the best to reason within?

Augustine teaches us that we must believe to understand. We must have a belief framework in which to reason correctly and find what we were made to love, to discover what we, as humans, are searching for. Ironically, Augustine asserts that it is reasonable to believe that we must first believe to reason correctly:

> And so, the prophet stated quite reasonably, *Unless you believe, you will not understand* (Is 7:9 LXX). There he undoubtedly distinguished these two and gave the counsel that we should believe first in order that we may be able to understand what we believe. Hence it was reasonably commanded that faith should precede reason. For, if this command is not reasonable it is, therefore, unreasonable. Heaven forbid! If, then, it is reasonable that faith precede reason with respect to certain great truths that cannot yet be grasped, however slight the reason is that persuades us to this, it undoubtedly also comes before faith.[7]

So it is reasonable to believe that we must have a framework of belief to understand. Sometimes we refer to this framework as "the faith." Thus, it is reasonable to believe that faith in "the faith" precedes reason.

Perhaps in reasoning this way, Augustine was recalling the days when he resolved "to live as a catechumen in the Catholic Church . . . until some kind of certainty dawned by which [he] might direct [his] steps aright."[8] He reasoned that belief in the church and the Scripture's authority might just provide the framework in which he could discover the right kind of understanding. As a pastor, he invited others to try on the faith to see if they could find some kind of clarity, livability, and healing. Would Christianity's churchly and scriptural authority help them find what they were longing for or lead them to the source of their desire?

Belief in the Testimony of an Authority

Augustine also came to realize that faith in some unproven assumptions or unobserved claims is necessary to function in everyday life. Why would the discovery of the most important, life-changing proofs be any different? He wrote in *Confessions*,

> So it was, Lord, that you began little by little to work on my heart with your most gentle and merciful hand, and dispose it to reflect how innumerable were

7. Augustine, *Letters* 120.3.
8. Augustine, *Confessions* 5.14.25.

> the things I believed and held to be true, though I had never seen them nor been present when they happened. How many truths there were of this kind, such as events of world history, or facts about places and cities I had never seen; how many were the statements I believed on the testimony of friends, or physicians, or various other people; and, indeed, unless we did believe them we should be unable to do anything in this life.[9]

Augustine first believed in the authority of Scripture and the church, even though all could not be proven to his satisfaction. There was no silver bullet argument or absolute certainty before he could believe. One seeking spiritual healing must trust in the authority without absolute confidence in the authority.

What Authority Should We Believe In?

But how do we know whether this authority should be trusted? Whom or what should we believe in? Peters answers this question, demonstrating that for Augustine, epistemology (how we know) and anthropology (who we are) are bound up together:

> To the question, "Which ultimate authority is it reasonable to trust?" Augustine responds that it is reasonable to trust as one's highest authority only the authority of the One who is the True Physician. The rationality of belief in God, then, which is essentially the rationality of trusting in the proper authority, is, quite astonishingly for a modern reader, a matter of the rationality of choosing the right physician. Hence the Augustinian canons for justified religious belief, far from being merely a matter of epistemology, are bound up with such questions as, "What are people for?" and even "Why are people so unhappy?"[10]

In this age in which the wounds of the soul are so prevalent, Augustine's pastoral advice is especially relevant. The framework that we should trust is the one with the power to cure our sin-sick souls. Why do we "run" the church in the first place if not to direct sinful and hurting people to the source of healing?

Yet it is not easy to trust in the healing power of the Scripture and the church. Augustine himself admits, "[My soul] could be healed only by believing, yet it shirked the cure for fear of believing what was false."[11] Ultimately

9. Augustine, *Confessions* 6.5.7.
10. Peters, *Logic of the Heart*, 74–75.
11. Augustine, *Confessions* 6.4.6.

Augustine believed and found healing in Jesus Christ and offered the medicine of the gospel to his congregation.

In the next chapter, we will expand on the therapeutic nature of pastoral ministry, especially as it relates to preaching. But healing does not need to wait until the Sunday sermon. Throughout the week, opportunities to apply the healing medicine of the gospel occur at every encounter with another human, whether during a hospital visit with an ailing church member or in an interaction with a staff member over their newly written job description. The hospital bed might seem to be a more obvious location for souls to be open to the gospel's therapy, but the office or the conference room can be a location for wounded souls to receive the healing balm of the gospel as well, if we open our eyes and ears to the longings of those seated across from us.

In his award-winning book *The Care of Souls: Cultivating a Pastor's Heart*, Harold L. Senkbeil emphasizes how important daily pastoral ministry is to healing preaching. A pastor's attentiveness to the souls he encounters increases the depth of his ministry to those wounded souls. In a chapter titled "The Cure of Souls," he writes,

> What makes for good public preaching makes for effective individual teaching. The pastor must first listen to the soul before he can minister to the soul. Since the condition of the soul is disclosed primarily by the heart, effective physicians of the soul need to polish their listening skills, opening up not merely their ears, but their hearts to the suffering of the soul as well. As much as humanly possible and as the Spirit leads your understanding, read their emotions. Get inside their skin, as it were, so you can comprehend not merely with your mind but your whole being the complexities of the soul's distress. Faithful pastoral care of the soul starts when one heart discloses itself to another heart—then the healing ministrations of God's word and sacraments may be most effectively applied.[12]

Preaching and administering the sacraments are most effective when the pastor practices soul cure throughout the week. Listening is key. Peterson counsels pastors to "unbusy" their lives to have the unhurried leisure to listen to others. He writes, "The question I put to myself is not 'How many people have you spoken to about Christ this week?' but 'How many people have you listened to in Christ this week?'"[13] Through slowing down and being attentive, daily pastoral ministry and administrative tasks move from simply running a church to curing souls.

12. Senkbeil, *Care of Souls*, 69.
13. Peterson, *Contemplative Pastor*, 21.

The Affections, the Will, and the Mind

I once preached a sermon series on the book of Revelation. When I was nearing the completion of the series, I asked my wife, Karen, what she thought of my exposition of Revelation. She responded rather bluntly: "You took all the emotions out of it."

In my defense, it was during the frenzy over Tim LaHaye and Jerry B. Jenkins's bestselling book series *Left Behind*. I was attempting to steer the congregation away from chasing after the latest evangelical fads and ground them prudently in the true message of the book of Revelation. But there's probably a more basic reason why I "took all the emotions out" of Revelation. In Bible college and seminary I had been formed by an overly rationalist epistemology and an underdeveloped anthropology that affected the way I preached. Too often I viewed people as Spock-like content processors and preaching as content dispensing. Further, some prominent preachers in my past had manipulated their congregation's emotions to get their desired outcome. C. G. Finney's pragmatic methodologies loomed large at the time, whether for taking up an offering, recruiting volunteers to fill the missing slots in the nursery, or getting sinners to walk down a red-carpeted aisle at invitation time. As a rejection of these emotional, pragmatic appeals, I had developed a preaching anthropology in which emotions or desires were mostly bad. The preacher's job was to fill the mind with content that in turn would move the will to act to overcome the emotions and get them in line.

More recently in my ministry experience, Augustine has helped me with this deficient view of pastoring and preaching. Augustine presents a much more humane and integrated perspective on how the will is moved and how people decide. He aims to appeal to the thick affections without superficially manipulating the thin emotions through cunning rhetorical flourishes. Perhaps I have been persuaded to Augustine's point of view partly because I have felt the difference that it makes in the lives of others and in my own life.

With the emergence of robotics and the development of artificial intelligence, it is more important than ever that we minister as fully human persons to people we regard as fully human. Unfortunately, we can slide into viewing church members as units used to accomplish ministry objectives and sermons as primarily content delivery. As an inheritor of the Enlightenment—even in the way my Christian college and seminary trained me in a baptized modern rationalism—I surmised that my will directed me primarily through rational deliberations. The mind grasped a propositional truth that in turn informed the will. The will would choose to resist evil passions. Of course, the Holy Spirit was involved, but in pastoring and preaching, I owned the responsibility of giving right content—"truth"—while avoiding emotional appeals.

Augustine offers us a theologically and pastorally reflective alternative on what a human is and how to minister to humans. Unlike his ancient philosophical interlocutors, Augustine was convinced that the affections compel the will and mind toward God. Human love drives the will toward the good and directs the mind toward true knowledge. In what follows, we will look at Augustine's pastoral perspective on the integrative relationship among the affections, the will, and the mind.

The Universal Desire for Happiness

First, Augustine agreed wholeheartedly with the classic consensus on the universal desire for happiness. The philosophers were united in their conviction that all people seek happiness, though they disagreed about what would lead to the good life. Incredibly—and humorously—in book 19 of *The City of God*, Augustine tallies up 288 different schools that could be created out of the various views on happiness. In the face of this plethora of views on what makes a person happy, Augustine never denied the validity of humanity's universal desire to achieve happiness and the legitimacy of attempting to discover the true source of happiness: "In the view of everyone who is at all capable of using reason, it is a certainty that all people want to be happy. But when, in their mortal weakness, they ask who is happy or what makes them happy, they give rise to a whole host of major controversies on which the philosophers have exhausted their energies and consumed their leisure."[14]

What truly makes a person happy plays a major role in Augustine's anthropology. The vision of what produces the good life determines how Augustine understands the relationship among the affections, the will, and the mind. Those of us trained in modern approaches to ministry were taught—sometimes implicitly, at other times overtly—to scorn or deny the desire for happiness or pursuit of the good life. Augustine took a different approach. He worked with the grain of the universal desire for happiness, as did Blaise Pascal, one of the most influential philosophers in the Augustinian tradition. Pascal wrote, "All men seek happiness. This is without exception. Whatever different means they employ, they all tend to this end. The cause of some going to war, and of others avoiding it, is the same desire in both, attended with different views. The will never takes the least step but to this object. This is the motive of every action of every man, even of those who hang themselves."[15]

14. Augustine, *City of God* 10.1.
15. Pascal, *Pascal's Pensées* (Trotter), 113 (thought no. 425).

But Augustine aimed at a better happiness, one that tapped into the truest human desire. As a shepherd of Christ's flock, the bishop of Hippo led his congregation to the green pastures and still waters of happiness. Whether one is motivating participants in a church council meeting or having lunch with a church member, an awareness of everyone's desire for happiness can turn routine ministry moments into opportunities to point people to the source of true joy.

Good Passions Moving a Good Will Toward the Good

Second, Augustine challenged the classical view of the relationship among the passions, the will, and the mind. Augustine claimed that for all their differences, the Stoics and the Platonists had a similar approach to the mind, the will, and the passions: Resist the passions—which are located primarily in the body—through a will directed by rational deliberation.[16] In contrast to this impassive mindset, Augustine presents a different view of what directs and drives the will. Augustine employs the Stoics' and Platonists' anthropological terms but redefines how they function and how they interact with one another.

In preaching the book of Revelation, I was attempting to get my congregation to make a rational decision that in turn would direct their will to overcome their far too easily manipulated emotions. As we will see, Augustine takes a more pastoral and integrated approach in his preaching, one that relates to people more holistically.

In breaking with the classical view of how the intellect, the will, and the passions relate to one another, Augustine imagines the emotions as a force in a rightly directed will. "Augustine broke with classical moral philosophy in attributing the desires and passions, which it relegated to the body and viewed merely as disturbances, to the will itself and gave them a positive role in directing the fallen will towards the good."[17] For Augustine, what matters is the answer to the question "To what end is the will directed?" A rightly directed will is a good will; a wrongly directed will is a bad will. In what follows, notice how seamlessly he moves between the will and the emotions. In his perspective, these are not parts of the human person that we can simply parse out and study but interlocking, symbiotic ways of understanding human nature.

> The important factor here is the quality of a person's will. If it is perverse, these emotions will be perverse; but, if it is right, they will be not only blameless but

16. Augustine, *City of God* 9.4.
17. Harrison, *Augustine*, 95.

> even praiseworthy. The will is involved in all of them; or, rather, they are all nothing more than modes of willing. For what are desire and joy but the will consenting to things that we want? And what are fear and grief but the will dissenting from things that we do not want? When the consent takes the form of seeking the things that we want, it is called desire; and when it takes the form of enjoying the things that we want, it is called joy. Similarly, when we dissent from something that we do not want to have happen, it is called fear; and when we dissent from something that actually does happen to us against our will, it is called grief. And in general, as a person's will is attracted or repelled in accord with the diversity of things that are pursued or avoided, so it is changed and turned into emotions of the one sort or the other.
>
> Therefore, the person who lives according to God and not according to man must be a lover of the good, and it follows that he will hate the evil.[18]

Carol Harrison comments on this text: "The passions are, in fact, all acts of will: desire and joy are acts of will in agreement with what we wish for; fear and grief are acts of will in disagreement with what we reject ([*City of God*] 14.6). So, all the passions might be rightly felt by a Christian: if his love, or will, is right he fears to sin, desires to persevere, feels pain over sin and gladness in good works."[19] The passions are not necessarily a force for evil. With the will, they can be rightly directed and can be a force for good. So Augustine replaces the classical moral philosophy that the happy life can be achieved through reason gaining control over bodily passions. Rather, the passions can drive the rightly aimed will toward the good.

Loving the Ultimate Good

Third, for Augustine the issue is not simply that the will should be directed toward the right thing or things to attain happiness. Two other issues are still in play: (1) Toward what end should we direct our will? (2) How can we move our will to that end? The affections are not simply a consequence of a will rightly directed toward the good. Rather, the passions move the will toward the right thing. Harrison suggests that "love, operating through the passions, therefore takes the place of reason in directing man's will towards God."[20] The loves, the passions, the longings, and the desires move the will. Augustine asserts that "it is not the person who merely knows the good that is justifiably called good; it is rather the person who loves the good."[21] Thus,

18. Augustine, *City of God* 14.6.
19. Harrison, *Augustine*, 94.
20. Harrison, *Augustine*, 95.
21. Augustine, *City of God* 11.28.

knowledge is not the primary mover of the will; rather, love moves or, perhaps better, draws the will toward the good. According to Augustine, "A soul is drawn by its love wherever it is drawn."[22] The ultimate good to whom we, as beings who are created in the image of God, are drawn is our creator, "whose eternity is true, whose truth is eternal, whose love is eternal and true, and who is himself the eternal, true, and beloved Trinity, in whom there is neither confusion nor separation. And the things that are below us would not exist at all, nor would they be shaped by any form, nor would they seek or hold to any order, if they had not been made by him who supremely is, who is supremely wise, and who is supremely good."[23]

The good will is directed, first and foremost, not toward the goods of creation but toward the wise and good one who created it. God is the source of all things and the source of all knowledge and wisdom. The good will is drawn to God by its love of him. Having an intellectual grasp of the good is insufficient if one does not love the good.

When we know this truth about God and people, we can see into the reality of things. That Christian brother or sister sitting beside us at the folding table with the plastic tablecloth draped over it longs for more than sister Agnes's famous casserole. Through genuine interest and meaningful conversation we can help them discover the nature of their true cravings and nudge their will toward what they hunger for above all else.

The Loving Will and the Willing Love

Fourth, Augustine viewed the will and love as deeply interrelated. "To will is not just to rationally deliberate and choose to act, rather it is to love something and to be moved to act on the basis of that love."[24] Augustine equates love with the will: "A right will, therefore, is a good love, and a perverse will is an evil love."[25] In *Augustine on the Will*, Han-luen Kantzer Komline explains masterfully, "Augustine did not believe that 'will' and 'love' are always distinct entities. In fact, he identified a 'good will' as 'love' (*caritas*). Furthermore, just as he identifies a good will with love, so he identifies the seat of good willing, the will, with the seat of loving, the heart." In other words, love and the will are deeply bound up in Augustine's anthropology. Komline continues to relate this view to the intellect:

22. Augustine, *City of God* 11.28.
23. Augustine, *City of God* 11.28.
24. Harrison, *Augustine*, 94–95.
25. Augustine, *City of God* 14.7.

> It is vital to see that Augustine, in terminology as well as in general tenor, saw the will as just as much a matter of love and the heart as it was of the intellect. . . . There is, indeed, a way in which Augustine unseats the intellect from its throne in common understandings of human identity. He accomplished this by linking the will (*uoluntas*) and loving and the heart more closely than anyone had before him. His view of will shows us that a person's heart, what a person loves, is at the core of who she is. He does this by relating love to the [will] in a new way.[26]

To will the good is more than a matter of choosing the right thing—it necessarily involves the heart and the mind pursuing the good alongside the will.

Love Seeking Understanding

Finally, none of this is to say that Augustine viewed knowledge and reasoning as insignificant. In the previous section, we devoted our focus to the relationship of faith and understanding. In brief, Augustine regarded the framework for rationality as vital for good understanding, and he considered love as the way to increased knowledge of the good.

> Of course, no one can love the good unless he in some sense knows it ([*On the Trinity*] 10.1.1)—and we have seen that Augustine held there were certain truths which are both innate to man's mind and made known to him through God's revelation of Himself in Scripture. But it is love which both increases this knowledge ([*Tractates on the Gospel of John*] 96.4) and enables man to act upon it and use it rightly. Nowhere is this more evident than in what Augustine has to say about the will, or love, as a weight, drawn by desire and longing towards the good.[27]

For Augustine the quest for knowledge could be styled "Love seeking understanding." The person who will discover true knowledge turns out to be the seeker who loves true knowledge. In our daily pastoral responsibilities, we create a learning community by focusing on leading our congregation to become a more loving community. Loving environments, rightly and gently guided, are best suited to become learning environments.

Administratively, things get done when we are drawn and driven by love for the good. Running the church becomes a matter of directing one another to the source of our true happiness. One of the most surprising things for me about the church where I currently serve as the pastor is that every

26. Komline, *Augustine on the Will*, 429–30.
27. Harrison, *Augustine*, 95–96.

administrative meeting—church council, worship committee, staff meeting, finance meeting, flower committee, and so on—begins with a heartfelt devotional and a time of meaningful prayer. I have never served in a church that gets as much done with as much love as this one. Believe it or not, administrative tasks can become opportunities to inflame within one another love for God.

Love as a Gift of Grace

We do not just work up this love for the good; rather, God draws us by his grace to himself through our loves. We were made to love God and neighbor, so God moves us toward our truest loves. Augustine compares love to a weight that pulls a body to its proper place. A fire's weight pulls it upward; a stone's weight drags it downward. Oil poured into water rises to the surface. Water poured into oil sinks below the oil. In these examples, a body or substance does not rest as long as it remains disordered, but it rests once it is ordered properly—when it settles into its true resting place. Augustine claims that love is his weight that carries him along. He prays that God's gift will move him upward toward God: "Your Gift sets us afire and we are borne upward; we catch his flame and up we go. In our hearts we climb those upward paths, singing the songs of ascent."[28] God's gift directs the will, turning it upward toward God. Yet the person on ascent toward God will not find complete rest until they reach the Lord's house, the eternal abode in the presence of God. "There shall a good will find us a place, that we may have no other desire but to abide there for ever."[29] The gift is the Holy Spirit who inspires love in us upward toward God. "Augustine's identification of love and the Holy Spirit (which seems to be original to him) implies that all love of God is from God, that man moves and delights in God because of God's gift and grace, and is thus drawn to God by God."[30]

Delight moves a person in a certain direction, toward the thing desired. "One only loves, after all, what delights one. *Take delight in the Lord* (Ps 37:4)."[31] Augustine uses the terms that we equate with "longing," "loving," "delighting in," and "desiring" interchangeably. Humans naturally take delight in what seems pleasurable, beautiful, and good—what they sense will lead toward their own happiness. They love and long for what they perceive

28. Augustine, *Confessions* 13.9.10.
29. Augustine, *Confessions* 13.9.10.
30. Harrison, *Augustine*, 96.
31. Augustine, *Sermons* 159.3 (italics original).

will bring them the highest delight. Only through grace is a person's will directed toward delight in God. In grace, God moves the will upward toward what the person desires—God himself. Grace inspires love toward God, turning the will toward delight in God.[32]

The fallen will bends away from God to other false sources of "delight." It loves self, not God. It is proud, not humble. People cannot attain the good through unaided efforts. They do not know or do good without grace. But through grace, the Holy Spirit directs the will toward true delight. As Augustine says, "Your Gift sets us afire and we are borne upward."[33] Harrison emphasizes humanity's need of God's grace: "The love with which man loves God is in fact the love of God Himself which he inspires in men's hearts through His Holy Spirit; of himself man can do nothing but sin."[34]

For now, the rightly directed will desires eternal rest with God. It sighs and longs for the future fulfillment of its delight. But desire now is not spent for nothing. This life expands our capacity to be filled with what we desire. Augustine explains,

> The entire life of a good Christian is a holy desire. What you desire, however, you don't yet see. But by desiring you are made large enough, so that, when there comes what you should see, you may be filled. For, if you wish to fill a purse, and you know how big what will be given you is, you stretch the purse, whether it is made of cloth or leather or anything else. You know how much you are going to obtain, and you see that your purse is small; by stretching it you make it that much larger. This is how God stretches our desire through delay, stretches our soul through desire, and makes it large enough by stretching it. Let us desire, then, brothers, because we have to be filled.[35]

Even unfulfilled desires are grace as God expands our capacity for love. Grace directs our will with longing for the fullness of God's eternal love.

The everyday words we use in pastoral ministry shape our community and the individuals among us. Our verbal expressions have the power to create a community directed toward the good. Or they can be like a needle that punctures a balloon, letting all the air and buoyancy out. Of course, we must use certain words in running the church, words like "mission," "vision," "strategy," "administration," "job descriptions," "expectations," "resources," "brand," and so on. Obviously, these words are necessary to run any organization. But their usage should pale in comparison to the number of times

32. Harrison, *Augustine*, 96.

33. Augustine, *Confessions* 13.9.10.

34. Harrison, *Augustine*, 100.

35. Augustine, *Homilies on the First Epistle of John* 4.6.

we use words like "love," "joy," "peace," "patience," "kindness," "generosity," "faithfulness," "gentleness," and "self-control"; or "beauty," "goodness," and "truth"; or "longing," "desiring," and "seeking"; or "loving God" and "loving others."

If I ever get a preaching do-over for the book of Revelation, I will take a different approach. Instead of throwing an exegetical bucket of cold water on parishioners' passions, or methodically presenting them the factual propositions that underlie Revelation, I would appeal to their deepest longings through the text, which would include their longing for God's reign, their desire to worship the worthy Lamb, their longing for answered prayer, their passion for God to set things right, their affections for the presence of God, and their yearning for shalom in a new heaven and new earth. I wouldn't attempt to throw a wet blanket on their desires; instead, I would move them to higher longings from deeper loves placed within them as humans created to love and worship God. By appealing to their loves, I am convinced that God's Spirit will open their minds to the truth of the book and draw their wills to himself.

While we do "manage" the church, equally vital are the practices of slowing, observing, listening, and being aware of the humans and the humanity in our orbit, those who are sitting in the meeting room with us, standing by the printer beside us, or passing by us as we walk up the stairs. What words can we say, inflections can we notice, or longings can we observe as we fellowship with parishioners and congregants? What are those things that can help us cooperate with the gift of God so that we can point the will of others toward the good and inflame their passion for knowing and loving the truth? How may we enter everyday moments—moments that are embedded in running a church—with an awareness of the relationship among the affections, the will, and the mind so that we may direct people to what they are truly longing for: God's love and a community of God's love? With an Augustinian anthropology, shepherding the church can become more than running a church.

Love as a Hermeneutical Principle

Before closing this chapter and moving on to preaching that heals souls, I want to make a comment on how love shapes our interpretation of Scripture in the church. In its weekly interactions and in doing the business of administration, the church needs to develop a loving posture to be a place of healing. When engaging in a Bible study or preparing to listen to a sermon, we may ask ourselves, "Is my aim to determine who is right and who is wrong, or am I trying to learn how to love God and others better in a way that is truer and more beautiful?" If people are lovers, then the primary aim of managing the church, studying the Bible, and preaching or listening to a sermon is to grow in love. So let's give some attention to love as a hermeneutical principle.

We know that where there is scriptural interpretation, there can be disagreements. And where there are disagreements over readings of the Bible, conflicts can arise. So the very thing that should bring deeper community becomes a source of division. How do we keep that from happening? Augustine advises that we interpret the Scriptures together "in the wide pastures of charity." He writes a prayer in *Confessions* regarding interpreting the early chapters of Genesis: "But as for those who feed on your [God's] truth in the wide pastures of charity, let me be united with them in you, and in you find my delight in company with them. Let us approach the words of your book together, and there seek your will as expressed through the will of your servant, by whose pen you have dispensed your words to us."[36]

The Scriptures are best understood and received in the context of a loving community where we show generosity toward other people's readings of the Bible. Even the way we interpret Scriptures—in our Sunday school classes, our small groups, our weekly Bible studies—can be a means for the cure of souls as we create loving interpretive communities. These types of gatherings open hearts to learn the truth—our minds simply work better when they experience love—because the aim of interpretation is love of God and love of one's neighbor.

In *Teaching Christianity*, Augustine claims that a person's understanding of a biblical text is a bad one if their reading of the text does not lead to the love of God and others: "So if it seems to you that you have understood the divine scriptures, or any part of them, in such a way that by this understanding you do not build up this twin love of God and neighbor, then you have not yet understood them."[37] If our interpretation does not lead us to love, then our reading of the text is insufficient!

When love is a guiding hermeneutical principle, the way we run the church does not become a test of orthodoxy, a tussle for the one right way to organize the church, or the biblical methodology to get work done; instead, running a church is accomplished by love and for love. The aim and practice of church administration is achieved in the wide pastures of charity for the purpose of shepherding the church members toward love.

36. Augustine, *Confessions* 12.23.32.

37. Augustine, *Teaching Christianity* 1.36.40.

Conclusion

Running the church does not have to be soul sucking. The daily administrative duties can be a means to lead people to happiness and human flourishing if we see people as lovers who believe and think. Understanding that human minds apprehend true knowledge and wisdom rightly when the will is aimed toward love of God and neighbor and moved by longings for the good, we should see administrative tasks and pastoral duties as opportunities to lead people toward their own good and happiness in God. We help them resist the urge for less and inspire a vision in them for more—more happiness, more flourishing, more of God. We rouse their desires for ultimate goods. In 1941, C. S. Lewis famously preached a sermon on our human desires that can be applied to our daily pastoral duties:

> If there lurks in most modern minds the notion that to desire our own good and earnestly to hope for the enjoyment of it is a bad thing, I submit that this notion has crept in from Kant and the Stoics and is no part of the Christian faith. Indeed, if we consider the unblushing promises of reward and the staggering nature of the rewards promised in the Gospels, it would seem that Our Lord finds our desires not too strong but too weak. We are half-hearted creatures, fooling about with drink and sex and ambition when infinite joy is offered us, like an ignorant child who wants to go on making mud pies in a slum because he cannot imagine what is meant by the offer of a holiday at the sea. We are far too easily pleased.[38]

Some pastors have become far too easily satisfied with making the mud pies of running a church and have invited the congregation to join in making them. Instead, we should use the opportunities in our daily activities to lead people to the healing waters, the calming breezes, and expansive visions of the ocean of God's beauty, goodness, and truth.

In the next chapter, we turn to seeing how an Augustinian anthropology relates to preaching as an act of curing souls. How do we preach a healing message to people, who are made to believe in order to understand and who must direct their wills toward the good in order to know the truth? Without manipulating their emotions, how do we preach to inflame their desires to apprehend and rest in God? How do we lead them on a pilgrimage to the sea of God's presence and God's love?

38. Lewis, *Weight of Glory*, 26.

FOUR

Preaching That Heals

And therefore if the head and body are to be well, you must begin by curing the soul; that is the first thing. And the cure, my dear youth, has to be effected by the use of certain charms, and these charms are fair words.

—Plato, *Charmides* 157a (trans. Jowett)

What after all am I, but someone needing to be set free with you, cured with you?

—Augustine, *Sermons* 9.10

There's nothing better, nothing more pleasant than to search through the divine treasure chest with nobody making a commotion; it's pleasant, it's good. But to preach, to refute, to rebuke, to build up, to manage for everybody, that's a great burden, a great weight, a great labor.

—Augustine, *Sermons* 339.4

Augustine had to "run" a church too. His typical responsibilities included overseeing various forms of charity and social welfare, hearing legal cases, preaching, leading liturgical rites, ransoming captives, and offering personal guidance to individuals.[1]

1. Kolbet, *Augustine and the Cure of Souls*, 10. Kolbet's work shaped much of the content in this chapter.

Curer of Souls

Yet Augustine's theological imagination enabled him to care for souls through these ministerial responsibilities. In *Augustine and the Cure of Souls: Revising a Classical Ideal*, Paul R. Kolbet explains,

> Augustine made these often-burdensome duties the subject of inquiry and developed a sophisticated pastoral theory in which these ministries of *care* could be understood as various expressions of more fundamental convictions regarding the soul's *cure*. Indeed, in Augustine's Latin, the word *cura* had two distinct but overlapping meanings. On the one hand, it meant "to be charged with administration." On the other hand, medically, it meant "healing treatment." In time, the *cura animarum* became synonymous with Christian ministry itself. For this reason, one seeking Augustine's advice could readily appeal to him as a "physician of the soul" (*medicum spiritalem*).[2]

Kolbet's thoughts on the way Augustine developed his approach to pastoral ministry as a work of healing supports points made in the previous chapter regarding opportunities for soul care amid administrative duties, but these thoughts also prepare the way for understanding Augustine's therapeutic approach to public oration. The pastors who are open to being agents of healing throughout the week, through personal interactions and administrative duties, prepare themselves to be agents of healing in the pulpit on Sunday morning.

As I write these words, it is Monday morning. Yesterday, just before our Sunday morning service, Anne, an eightysomething saint, shared a prayer request for her dear friend who was having a partial hip replacement and the removal of a tumor. As I listened to Anne's request, I looked deeply into her eyes, trying to hear her heart. I wanted her genuine affections for her friend to heal me and form me. This kind of love is characteristic of Anne. Her affections are rightly directed to care for people. Her will is aimed toward loving her neighbor out of her love for God. She thinks pure thoughts of kindness toward her loved ones. She had no idea that she was pastoring me. I hope that my genuine desire to learn from her and be formed by her well-ordered loves ministered healing to her as well.

These simple but meaningful encounters throughout the week prepare my affections, will, and mind to preach the Scriptures on Sunday morning. They are therapeutic moments, not heavy burdens—although if I am not careful to attend to these moments rightly, they can seem like duties to check off on my overwhelming to-do list. Instead, these encounters are a life-giving source,

2. Kolbet, *Augustine and the Cure of Souls*, 10 (italics original).

shaping me for preaching with a rightly ordered pastor's heart. These are God-ordered moments available to us to cure others and be cured by others through God. Preaching extends these healing moments to the gathered people of God.

Augustine preached therapeutically and was grounded in his view of what a human is; how the affections, will, and cognition interact with one another; and how faith relates to understanding. To review, Augustine did the following:

- *Placed faith before understanding.* We must believe to understand. We should entrust ourselves to the authority that brings true healing to our souls.
- *Viewed humans as lovers*—lovers of God and neighbor.
- *Innovated on the classical perspective of the relationship among a human's mind, will, and affections.* The affections drive the will toward the telos of loving God and others, which in turn influences the way people think.

These theologically formed perspectives shaped the way he pastored and preached to humans. His preaching was therapeutic, rightly directing the loves toward God and neighbor.

Preaching as Therapy

It is well known that Augustine was educated in the classical rhetorical arts. He excelled as a practitioner and professor of rhetoric beyond his classmates and teachers. His rhetorical skills catapulted him beyond the margins of the Roman Empire to its very center. He was ultimately appointed to the influential position of professor of rhetoric in the city of Milan. Peter Brown, Augustine's most recognizable biographer, explains the significance of Augustine's prominent role: "As the Imperial court resided in Milan, this was an important appointment. A professor of rhetoric would deliver the official panegyrics on the Emperor and the consuls of the year."[3] Perhaps we could think of Augustine as the emperor's publicist and promoter of his policies. Suffice it to say, he understood the art of classical rhetoric.

In the 390s, after his ordination as a priest and then as a bishop, Augustine reimagined the purpose and use of rhetoric. A primary function of rhetoric according to classical philosophy is to bring human healing and flourishing.

3. Brown, *Augustine of Hippo*, 58.

The ideal classical orator cures souls. This notion predates Augustine, and Christianity for that matter. Kolbet asserts, "Indeed, the ideal of an orator who cures the souls of hearers in the same way that a physician cures the body both preceded Christianity and influenced its earliest expressions."[4] The classical view that a rhetor's words have the power to cure souls influenced Augustine's understanding of preaching. Yet Augustine reconceived the healing power of rhetoric in the light of the revelation of Scripture. Augustine baptized rhetoric's function in the waters of the mediatory work of Jesus Christ.

Thus, for Augustine, the preacher's words convey therapeutic power. The act of preaching cures souls. Yet Augustine did not view himself as the healer. For Augustine, Jesus Christ is the healer and a teacher, imparting healing wisdom to disordered humans. The healing power resides in Jesus Christ, not the rhetorical arts. Commenting on Augustine as pastor, Gerald Bray notes that, as a preacher, Augustine saw himself as "the means by which the people were fed, but he was not the food himself, just as the doctor is the dispenser of medicine but does not himself have its curative effects."[5] Like a doctor, the preacher dispenses the curative power of Jesus Christ.

Jesus Christ, the Doctor and the Cure

Better yet, Jesus Christ is both the doctor and the cure. As the wisdom of God, Jesus Christ's teaching heals souls weighed down by sin's sickness. "In this way, 'Wisdom adapted its healing art to our wounds by taking on a human being' and becoming 'itself both the physician (*medicus*) and the medicine (*medicina*).'"[6] In life and preaching, Jesus Christ is the medic and the medicine. He heals through the lively preaching of the word in the gathered congregation. Jesus Christ is the doctor, and he applies the cure in the church.

"Augustine's favorite—or at least, most frequent—image of Christ was as a medical doctor," claims William Harmless.[7] In Augustine's preaching, the references to Jesus Christ's healing ministry are too many to list here. It must suffice to look at a sermon that got at the source of all human maladies: pride. In an exposition on John 6:15–44, Augustine asserts, "The origin of all sicknesses is pride, because the origin of all sins is pride. . . . Why does wickedness abound? Because of pride. Treat the pride, and there will be no wickedness. So then, in order that the cause of all sicknesses, that is pride,

4. Kolbet, *Augustine and the Cure of Souls*, 7.

5. Bray, *Augustine on the Christian Life*, 176.

6. Kolbet, *Augustine and the Cure of Souls*, 142, quoting Augustine, *Teaching Christianity* 1.14.13.

7. Harmless, *Augustine in His Own Words*, 140.

might be treated, the Son of God came down and was made humble."[8] Jesus Christ, the great physician, heals pride by applying to humanity the cure of his own humility. Rowan Williams adds, "By incarnation, death, and resurrection, the Word creates a relation between himself and the human race that brings all human experience within the scope of healing and restoration."[9] Preaching with a therapeutic aim has restorative power.

The Church, a Hospital for Healing

For Augustine, this healing and restoration occurs most holistically in the church. According to Harmless, "Augustine linked the image of Christ the Doctor with the image of the Church as a hospital."[10] In a homily on John 8:3–36, Augustine concludes with the healer and the place of healing: "Let us beseech the healer of our wounds, let us be carried to the inn to be healed. . . . So then, brothers and sisters, the Church, too, in this age, in which the wounded man is being looked after, is the inn for us on our journey; but to the same Church is reserved the inheritance of the one who possesses it above."[11] The church is an inn—a hospital, if you will—in which we recuperate on our journey to our eternal inheritance in the heavenly city. The same physician who will finally heal all our ills in our heavenly home today works among us to bind our wounds and treat our pride. The church is on a lifelong journey of healing as our redeemed hearts travel along the path to the new heaven and new earth.

Preaching is a healing act aimed at integrating the affections, the will, and the mind toward the love of God, instructing the whole person to love God humbly and holistically. Jesus works through the congregation as the whole Christ, using the preacher's words to heal the congregation of pride, put them back together, and draw them to the love of God. Preaching guides listeners along the path to an integrated life as they are restored to their truest humanity: as people who love God holistically with affection, volition, and cognition.

The journey toward holistic healing is along the path of the affections; the sermon should appeal to the affections and habituate the heart toward the love of God. J. Patout Burns Jr. asserts the aim of Augustine's preaching: "Augustine's objective in preaching was to move his hearers as much as to instruct them."[12] To instruct and challenge are vital components of preaching,

8. Augustine, *Homilies on the Gospel of John* 25.16.
9. Williams, "Augustine's Christology," 181.
10. Harmless, *Augustine in His Own Words*, 144.
11. Augustine, *Homilies on the Gospel of John* 41.13.
12. Burns, *Augustine's Preached Theology*, 22.

but the pathway to an integrative life begins with the affections. Soul cure starts with the desires.

Preaching from the Heart to Hearts

A few weeks before writing this chapter, I decided on a certain Sunday morning (in 2024) to change the sermon I had prepared, preach from my heart, and aim at the affections of the congregation. At that time, I was making my way through a series on the book of Acts. The text on the Sunday that I called an audible was Acts 20. I had prepared a sermon with eight points. (I know better than to have that many points, but sometimes I break the rules.) They were clear and relevant points that accurately represented the exegesis of the text. But my heart ached because I could not fit my passion for that text into those points. I felt the message burning in my heart, but I could not communicate the truth I knew about that text within the confines of my outline.

At my ordination on July 30, 1989, I preached from Acts 20 the truth of Paul's farewell words to the Ephesian elders. That night, I encountered Paul's impassioned words in a way that has held true through my years of ministry. My passion for that text has only grown since preaching it thirty-five years ago. Additionally, on that Sunday morning in 2024, Paul's warnings to the Ephesian elders had particular relevance to our congregation. In our denomination, "savage wolves [had] come in among [us] . . . from [our] own number . . . distort[ing] the truth in order to draw away disciples after them" (Acts 20:29–30 NIV).

Instead of grinding my way through the outline, I decided to preach from my affections by telling my story, relating it to the text's first-century story, and connecting the truth of the text to our church's twenty-first-century story. Indeed, I instructed the congregation with an accurate exposition of the text. But more than that, they were moved. By tapping into my own shepherd-shaped affections, I appealed to the flock's affections and moved their desires toward a love of God's truth. I'm still learning that consistently appealing to the heart through impassioned preaching of story habituates the heart toward a whole and integrated life.

I'm glad I made the change that Sunday morning. I preached the text, but I didn't take "all the emotion out of it." I discovered the Holy Spirit–inspired heart of the text, found the same passion inside of me, and then moved the affections of my hearers.

A retired minister in the congregation wrote my wife and me the following note the week after the sermon:

Hey Mark and Karen
There have been several occasions at Memorial when I (and others) have felt mightily the presence of the Holy Spirit
None compare to This past Sunday
Thank you for the Role you played in it
Love you both[13]

The Holy Spirit and the Whole Worship Service

Oftentimes the Holy Spirit illuminates our minds to the truth of a text through moving our affections. Augustine understood the role of the Holy Spirit in healing and transforming our affections. In homily 97 of the *Homilies on the Gospel of John*, Augustine states, "This very Holy Spirit, then, both teaches believers now as many spiritual things as one can grasp and inflames their hearts with greater desire, if someone is making progress in that charity whereby he both loves what he knows and desires what must yet be known."[14] The Holy Spirit works through the affections to teach and to create desire for greater learning.

Kolbet weaves together human desire, the Holy Spirit, scriptural preaching, and the sacramental life of the church found in Augustine:

> It is important to note that scripture is no *deus ex machina* in this process of renewal, as if it could mechanistically cure the soul as a kind of efficient cause. In Augustine's homiletic practice, scripture maintains a necessary place within the organic whole of God's larger economy, which includes the entire ecclesial life of the Church. God's Word extends its curative presence into the world through the Holy Spirit's use of the whole sacramental life of the Church, which includes baptism and Eucharist. Scripture's efficacy in healing the affections of the heart derives from the Holy Spirit's use of it. Augustine preached to his congregation, "We cannot love God except through the Holy Spirit."[15]

Notice that the retired pastor wrote that Karen and I played a "Role in it." The other elements of the service—the ones that move the heart and mind—are vital to God's work in the sermon. The sermon is only a part of the service. An integrative and holistic approach to the sermon and the other liturgical elements in the service open hearts and minds to the word preached. The pastor can habituate the congregation toward opening their affections to the movement of God throughout the worship service. The freedom to share my

13. Personal letter to the author, September 21, 2025.
14. Augustine, *Homilies on the Gospel of John* 97.1.
15. Kolbet, *Augustine and the Cure of Souls*, 192.

affections for the text and for God's truth was therapeutic for me, but it was also a healing experience for the congregation. We encountered the medic and the medicine in the gathered body of Christ.

Healing and Humility

Aware of the healing power of preaching in the gathered congregation, Augustine cultivated in his hearers the humble disposition of a patient. Kolbet explains, "They should . . . behave more like patients who agree to be cared for by doctors, trusting that any painful treatments would be aimed at their disease rather than themselves."[16] To be healed, the congregation must be taught to examine the raw responses of their hearts to Scriptures to see their true spiritual states and what they really believe. Kolbet claims that Augustine felt that the "emotional responses" to sermons were better indicators of "the basic doctrines of the soul" than "public statements."[17] If a congregant wants to know what they really believe, or better yet, their actual spiritual health, then they should monitor their emotional responses to the sermons. Concluding sermon 59, Augustine sums up the diagnostic work done by his listeners: "You have dug very deep to pull up hatred of your enemies from your heart."[18] The Holy Spirit helps the listener diagnose the state of their affections so that they can offer their heart to the Lord for healing.

As a young minister, I had a difficult time diagnosing the condition of my heart. My affections often seemed fragmented and dis-integrated. Eventually I came to believe that my emotions were like gauges on my dashboard that could indicate the condition of my spiritual life. A glowing, red check engine light would alert me to look under the hood and see what's going on.

At that time, I journaled my prayers, so at the end of my prayer time, I would sit, listen, and do diagnostic work on my affections. To do this, I would write the following words on a yellow pad:

- Mad
- Sad
- Bad
- Glad

Then I would sit quietly, asking the Holy Spirit to search my heart.

16. Kolbet, *Augustine and the Cure of Souls*, 187.
17. Kolbet, *Augustine and the Cure of Souls*, 188.
18. Augustine, *Sermons* 49.10.

- Mad: Was I angry? Whom was I angry at? What was making me mad?
- Sad: Was I feeling down or depressed? What was I unhappy about? What was the source of my sadness?
- Bad: Was I feeling lonely, anxious, or overwhelmed? Was I tempted to sin?
- Glad: Was I feeling happy? What was I looking forward to? What was bringing me joy?

This was a very important exercise in my spiritual healing and development. Perhaps we could preach with these emotions and questions in mind. Further, what difference might it make if we teach our listeners to allow the Spirit-inspired Scriptures to do this type of diagnostic work on their feelings and desires? The result may be that through such diagnostic efforts, the Holy Spirit will do his healing and restorative work through the preaching of the word.

The church is a hospital for the weary, broken, and ailing. Though the diagnosis and treatment that come through the preaching of the word may feel invasive or cause pain, the goal is healing and restoration. Liturgies and preaching will combine to rehabilitate and rehabituate the patient toward healing if the preacher and listener engage their agencies in the healing process. Augustine reminds his listeners of the goal of sermonic therapy and the promise of the curative power of Scripture:

> Therefore, brothers and sisters, what calls for all our efforts in this life is the healing of the eyes of our hearts, with which God is to be seen. It is for this that the holy mysteries are celebrated, for this that the word of God is preached, to this that the Church's moral exhortations are directed, those, that is, that are concerned with the correction of our carnal desires, the improvement of our habits, the renunciation of this world, not only in words but in a change of life. Whatever points are made by God's holy scriptures, this is their ultimate point, to help us purge that inner faculty of ours from that thing that prevents us [from] beholding God.[19]

Currently my wife, Karen, is going to physical therapy three times a week for her shoulder. The pain she experiences aims to heal and strengthen. The exercises she engages in during the week habituate her toward health. Perhaps we could think of the sermon and liturgies as habituating the affections toward health, restoring and strengthening passions toward the love of the healer, moving the will toward true health, and opening the mind to curative wisdom. In this way, preaching cures souls.

19. Augustine, *Sermons* 88.5.

Healing in the Local Ministry

A preaching mentor once warned me, "You have to let go of your darlings." Darlings are those points, illustrations, or comments that do not drive the thesis of the sermon but that you love and have a difficult time letting go of. Commenting on Augustine's approach to preaching, Gerald Bray writes, "Whatever approach a preacher adopted, he was always to make sure that he was communicating with his audience." We might get more specific: Not some imaginary audience. Not his seminary professors. Not amateur theologians on social media. Not his own tastes and aesthetics. Not what may make himself look good. Bray adds, "Everything he said and did had to serve the ministry and not draw undue attention to himself."[20] Speakers must let go of their darlings to minister to the people in front of them. When it comes to preaching, what matters most is the congregation sitting in front of us. Our desire for the healing of those people in that place should move us to let go of our darlings.

Right now, as I lift my eyes to the wall in front of me, I see one single verse written in large letters: "Keep watch over yourselves and over all the flock, of which the *Holy Spirit* has made you overseers, to shepherd the church of *God* that he obtained with the blood of his own *Son*" (Acts 20:28 NRSVue; italics added).

As mentioned before, I preached on this text in 1989 for my ordination sermon. The part of the verse that catches my attention today is "of which the Holy Spirit has made you overseers." That flock. That specific localized part of the whole church. Not the flock in New York City, or Athens, Ohio, or Sarasota, Florida, or Minneapolis, Minnesota, or Jackson, Missouri, or Dallas, Texas, or Nephi, Utah, or Seattle, Washington. Augustine developed his ministry approach through biblical and theological reflection in a specific locality. He was Augustine of *Hippo*. Not Rome. Not Milan. But Hippo. Kolbet emphasizes this point: "Despite the astonishing manner in which Augustine towers over history and casts an unusually immense shadow, he truly had a local context and *all* of his thoughts and feelings grew organically out of the actual life he lived."[21] The souls he set out to cure in his preaching—not by himself but as an instrument used by Christ—were specific souls, in a certain time, in a particular place.

Though Augustine was aware of the cultural shifts and philosophical trends that affected his known world—see his grasp and critique of the Greco-Roman social imaginary in *The City of God*—he addresses larger cultural narratives

20. Bray, *Augustine on the Christian Life*, 181.
21. Kolbet, *Augustine and the Cure of Souls*, 9.

as a shepherd of a localized flock. He had experienced the center of the Roman world in Milan, but "from 396 until his death in 430, Augustine was bishop of Hippo, a medium-sized port city on the North African coast. . . . Beyond that however, he did not venture. . . . The greatest theologian of the Western church never went anywhere further than Carthage during his tenure as a bishop, though he kept in touch with the wider world through his correspondence."[22]

We must study the larger culture and engage with the wider world. Augustine did. But when it comes time to preach, let us do diagnostics and apply the healing truth on the wounds of the congregation that is present with us and understand how the historical, international, national, and cultural trends influence the desires and frustrations of our specific local church, those people making eye contact with us during the worship service. Years ago, I read something along the lines of "Just because is it raining in South Barrington [the location of an influential megachurch at that time in Illinois] doesn't mean that you put on a raincoat in your hometown." Just because it works in one place, does not mean that we mimic it in our town. Each of us is a specific preacher ministering in the climate of a particular congregation. The ailments in our congregation are common to humans, but the maladies occur under the condition of our hometowns. The spiritual treatment must fit the parish's ailments.

Augustine realized how the culture shaped the social imaginary and the inner world of his hearers: "Every human being, wherever he or she is born, learns the tongue of that country, or district, or civic community, and is imbued with the customs and way of life proper to the place." He inquires how the child would be nurtured in a particular spiritual disease: "How, for instance, could a child born among pagans avoid paying cult to a stone idol, when his parents have trained him in that form of worship? In that milieu he heard his earliest words; he sucked in that falsehood with his mother's milk."[23] Think of how family origins affect the spiritual health of a person. The preacher must be aware of how his parishioners have been shaped by their family backgrounds. To understand this, shepherds must know their sheep, love their sheep, and listen to their sheep. As the saying goes, "A shepherd must smell like sheep." Why do the shepherds smell like sheep? Because they have been with the sheep in their homes, at their jobs, in their world. Augustine preached two or three times a week for more than thirty years to the congregation in Hippo.[24] He knew their spiritual illnesses, and he learned how to apply the balm of the gospel to their specific ills.

22. Bray, *Augustine on the Christian Life*, 141–42.
23. Augustine, *Expositions of the Psalms* 64.6.
24. Burns, *Augustine's Preached Theology*, 2.

As we have heard, to preach well the pastor must exegete the text, but just as importantly, the pastor must exegete the congregation. When knowledge of the word combines with knowledge of the people, the healing potential of the sermon increases exponentially.

Curing Souls Through Authentic Preaching

Manuscripted, Memorized, and Impromptu Preaching

On one occasion Augustine had prepared to preach on a particular psalm. The lector mistakenly read Psalm 139 instead of the psalm that Augustine had prepared to speak on. How did Augustine respond to this error? He preached extemporaneously on Psalm 139. With no notes and no preparation, he preached from his heart, trusting God for strength and the presence of mind to preach on that text.[25]

This is an extreme example of the impromptu nature of Augustine's preaching. Augustine believed that preaching should be from the heart, a response to the congregation. He prepared deeply and diligently for his sermons, but he did not write out notes or memorize the sermon. No three propositional points and a poem for Augustine. Augustine surmised that those who wrote out their sermons and delivered them verbatim did not have the freedom, as he did, to respond to the congregation and change some aspect of their content or delivery. Augustine pointed this out in book 4 of *Teaching Christianity*: "Now this is something that is simply not in the power of those who recite sermons they have prepared and learned by heart, word for word."[26] The same could be said of those who read their sermons word for word. There's something between them and the congregation. They are not fully inhabiting the preaching moment.

Augustine hid his sermon's structure, sometimes artlessly, so as not to appear pretentious. It could seem that he was meandering about in his sermon, but he always had a deeper structure and clear aim. His preaching was masterfully down to earth.[27] As noted above, he could be critical of those who wrote out their sermons and read them or memorized them. As a preaching pastor who was attuned to the reactions of his congregation and responded accordingly, he valued spontaneity. He could do this because he "was conscious of being a channel for conveying God's Word to the people."[28] Further, he preached not from some tedious word search but from the fire in his breast,

25. Bray, *Augustine on the Christian Life*, 176; Burns, *Augustine's Preached Theology*, 3.
26. Augustine, *Teaching Christianity* 4.10.25.
27. Kolbet, *Augustine and the Cure of Souls*, 175.
28. Bray, *Augustine on the Christian Life*, 174.

as he explains in book 4 of *Teaching Christianity*: "As for the grand manner of speaking, it is as far removed as can be from this moderate kind, being not so much a matter of elegantly stylish language as of the impetuous expression of very deep feelings. . . . It is sufficient, you see, for the subject which engages it that suitable words, rather than being picked by the deliberation of the tongue, should follow upon the ardor of the breast."[29]

For Augustine, the subject matter and the passion of the soul drove the word choice. His word choice ran along the contours of the text. That is, the humble words of the text gave him his preaching vocabulary. If his own words happened to attain to elegance and beauty, so be it. It was enough to convey the meaning of the text with great passion.

We have Augustine's sermons written down because stenographers recorded them, not because Augustine wrote them out. It's a wonderful gift to have his sermons passed down to us in writing. Yet because of Augustine's prayerful preparation and dynamic presentation—not to mention his background as a teacher of rhetoric—his written sermons do not do justice to what it would have been like to hear his delivery live. We miss his pace, dramatic pauses, gestures, vocal inflection, and facial expressions.[30] For Augustine, a mechanical delivery was the death of a sermon. Dynamism and spontaneity enlivened the sermon. His lively sermons engaged the hearers and increased the intimacy between them. We can hear the urgency of his affectionate engagement and closeness in the following comments on Ezekiel 3:18–19, addressed directly to his congregation: "What, after all, do I want? What do I desire? What am I longing for? Why am I speaking? Why am I sitting here? What do I live for, if not with this intention that we should all live together with Christ? That is my desire, that's my honor, that's my most treasured possession, that's my joy, that's my pride and glory. But if you don't listen to me and yet I have not kept quiet, then I will deliver my soul. But I don't want to be saved without you."[31]

In the first steps of my own preaching journey, Augustine's directives toward impromptu preaching would have scared me to death, and even today, they make me nervous to some extent. Or, better, they challenge me.

When I first started preaching as a church planter, I wrote out every word of the sermon. In my delivery of the sermon, I read the manuscript word for word while sitting on a stool behind a music stand—barely looking up at the congregation and making only minimal gestures, if any. Eventually, I was able to stand up to preach. Next, I tried a few awkward gestures. Later,

29. Augustine, *Teaching Christianity* 4.20.42.
30. Harmless, *Augustine in His Own Words*, 124; Burns, *Augustine's Preached Theology*, 3.
31. Augustine, *Sermons* 17.2.

I ventured out away from the music stand. By the time I left that pastorate fifteen years later, I used only my Bible and a few notes. No music stand or pulpit, only a stool—not to sit on but to set my Bible and notes on. I wanted nothing between me and the congregation and desired to make eye contact with them.

At my present pastorate, I stand behind a rather large pulpit and preach from a manuscript. I don't practice the sermon much, but I do read through the notes several times before I preach it. I don't think the issue is whether I have notes or a manuscript. In the spirit of Augustine, I preach from the heart with passion, remaining flexible and responsive to the congregation. I never want to go through the motions or distance myself from the flock.

The legendary homiletics professor Robert Smith Jr. had a unique way of teaching his students how to preach spontaneously. He had an exercise called "fishbowl." He would write the word "reader" and a biblical text on a piece of paper and the word "preacher" and the same biblical text on another piece of paper. Then he would place those and blank pieces of paper in the fishbowl. Each homiletics student in the class would then draw one piece of paper out of the fishbowl. The student who picked out the "reader" paper had to walk to the front of the class, read the text, and pray. The student who drew out the "preacher" paper had to prepare his sermon on the biblical text while the reader walked to the front of the class, read the text, and prayed. That's scary, but effective.

My son, Colton, was one of Robert Smith's students and also his graduate assistant. Colton got "fishbowled" two times in a row. He received the following advice from Smith: "Trust the God of your mind and the mind that God gave you." Colton never got over that advice. It changed him in a positive and profound way.

Recently I sat behind Colton as he preached a sermon from his heart to the congregation I pastor. Our congregation was deeply affected by Colton's message on the good shepherd. He preached it deliberately, powerfully, and therapeutically. He did not miss a beat. He trusted his mind. The congregation felt the benefit of his heartfelt preaching.

To "trust the God of your mind and the mind that God gave you," I would add a statement about the "heart." Trust the God who renews your heart by the Holy Spirit, and trust the heart that God is cultivating so that you may shepherd well from the pulpit the flock of which the Holy Spirit has made you an overseer. Whether in the study or in the pulpit, we need to risk spontaneity and responsiveness in order to be used by Christ to heal the sheep.

The issue is not so much whether the sermon is impromptu or rehearsed, or whether you have notes or a manuscript. In fact, Augustine admitted that "there are, of course, some people who can declaim and enunciate well, but cannot think up and compose anything to say and declaim. But if they take things that have been written eloquently and wisely by others, and proffer them to the people, provided they have that role to play, they are not acting improperly." He explains why it is not "stealing" to preach the words of others: "Those who steal, after all, are purloining what does not belong to them; but God's word does belong to those who do what he tells them. In fact, it's the man who speaks well and lives badly that really speaks words that do not belong to him."[32] Perhaps the question is "Are we living the words that we are speaking, and are the words alive in us?" Again, do we know the sheep? Do we love them? Are we responsive to the congregation in front of us? Do we love those sheep and minister the Scriptures to their needs?

Let's ask ourselves, "If our congregation didn't show up, would it make any difference in our delivery? How healing can the preaching be if the congregation's presence doesn't matter?" Aware of the whole Christ at the preaching event, we should engage the congregation's affections, will, and cognition with our own affections, will, and cognition, enlivened by the presence of the Spirit of Christ. Such engaged preaching enhances the healing power of preaching moments. It did for Augustine; it will for us.

The Teaching and Preaching Spirit

To preach to the whole person in a healing way, preachers must be convinced that the spirit in which they preach matches or exceeds the importance of their content and rhetoric.

At Notre Dame I took a patristic exegesis course with Augustine scholar John Cavadini. As I listened to John's lectures on Augustine's exegetical methodology and pedagogical reflections, I scribbled notes and quotes from him throughout my copy of *Teaching Christianity*. Here are some of my favorite quotes related to our teaching spirit:

"It's possible to translate Scripture into the wrong spirit by overemphasizing the eloquence of the translation."

"You don't just teach information; you teach the spirit in which you teach."

"An academic institution teaches by its spirit."

32. Augustine, *Teaching Christianity* 2.28.62. Of course, today we must avoid plagiarism, and even more importantly, we must avoid being dishonest with the congregation and ourselves. Pretending we are preaching our own message when we are just reading someone else's sermon misses the mark of authenticity that we are aiming at in this chapter.

"Your spirit in teaching is what is important; it is also important in what learning culture you create."

"This kind of speaking transforms pride into charity. Not in an anti-intellectual way, but what matters above all is the spirit in which you teach and learn."

"Teach in a way that is governed by the spirit Scripture teaches."

"Augustine is teaching a different spirit of teaching."

The way Cavadini taught enlarged my imagination and inflamed my desires for communicating Scripture with a disposition that accords with Christ's humility, wisdom, and love. The emphasis on the spirit of the teacher resonated with me. In accord with Augustine's burden, we could easily replace the word "teaching" with "preaching" and the terms "culture" and "academic institution" with "church": A church preaches by its spirit.

Humility in Preaching as a Way of Healing

The eloquence that Augustine desired to teach is not one of style or form but of the spirit. It's fine if you can learn the rules of rhetoric, but it's better if you can catch the spirit of Scripture. In book 2 of *Teaching Christianity*, Augustine instructs his readers that the wise rhetor teaches with a cruciform spirit, communicating by his disposition the sacrificial love and self-giving humility of Jesus Christ. Augustine urges preachers to come to Jesus and inhabit his gentle and humble spirit (Matt. 11:28–30) so that they are not being puffed up by their knowledge but being built up in love (1 Cor. 8:1).[33]

Augustine modeled the way of humility in the way he preached. It is surprising how often in his sermons Augustine models humility by admitting that he is not sure about his understanding of a text or by asking the congregation to think with him through the interpretation of a Scripture. Charles Kim, who believes that humility is central to Augustine's theology of preaching, explains, "The term *via humilitatis* comes from Augustine himself, which he says Christ demonstrated and taught his followers. The preacher proclaims the truths found in the scriptural text and exemplifies the *via humilitatis* before the gathered church in his speech. The hearers learn to imitate from their preacher the virtue of humility and turn inwards themselves to find Christ the teacher. The preacher relies on God in the gift [of] grace to work on the inside of the hearers through the words of Scripture and the preacher."[34]

33. Augustine, *Teaching Christianity* 2.41.62.
34. Kim, *Way of Humility*, xli.

The humility of the preacher models the way of the humble Savior revealed in the humility of Scripture. Thus, the humble Christ—as the whole Christ—teaches the congregation the way that leads to healing through the path of humility. Kim continues, "From one vantage point, Augustine appears to be the teacher for the congregation. At a deeper level, the aim of Augustine is to lead the whole body of Christ in the Church, to a vision of the humble Christ, who is the true teacher. The language of school becomes critical for the gathered body in the moment of the sermon."[35]

The spirit of humility in preaching goes beyond mere modeling. The meek disposition and style of the preacher lead the congregation to the therapeutic teaching of Christ's own humility. Augustine sets forth a reason that God often heals pride through a humble preacher: "So the doctor cures the disease with its contrary: a cold condition with hot aids, a hot state with cold compresses, a dry state with moist dressings, a moist condition with dry ones. So if we see the art of medicine curing a patient by the application of contraries, it's not surprising if we who were sick with human pride are cured by the humility of God. And so it was safer and sounder for the Lord to gain an orator through a fisherman than a fisherman through an orator."[36] God often heals the pride of the orator through the humility of the fisherman. The motto of the university where I teach is "training champions for Christ." I tell my ministerial students, "Humble pie is the breakfast of pastoral champions." A soul nourished on the humility of Christ shows others the way of Christ.

The humble kindness expressed in the eyes of the preacher, or the haughty disgust on his face, communicates clearly even if his words are attempting to send a different message: "For this reason, audiences respond to the spirit of the person speaking to them more than to his actual words. People are turned on when 'they see those minds which are trying to affect them kindled by the same fire.'"[37] Gerald Bray points out that "Augustine's colleague and biographer Possidius wrote that although people who read his theological works profited from them, 'those who could hear him speak in church profited still more.'"[38] No doubt Augustine was a master at the turn of phrase. Few exceeded his facility with words, but even his word choice flowed out of a humble spirit enlivened with love for God and neighbor. This may be another reason why he preferred more extemporaneous preaching. In the words of one

35. Kim, *Way of Humility*, xlvi.

36. Augustine, *Sermons* 341.4.

37. Bray, *Augustine on the Christian Life*, 180–81, quoting Augustine, *On the Catechizing of the Uninstructed* 2.7.

38. Bray, *Augustine on the Christian Life*, 174, quoting Possidius, *Vita Augustini* 31.244.

of my seminary buddies (who was asked to manuscript his sermon), "Brother, you can't put fire on paper."

What does it take for the preacher to ready himself to preach? What does he do to prepare his spirit to preach on Sunday? An older pastor who had been seasoned by years of pastoral ministry was once asked, "How long did it take you to prepare that sermon?" He responded wryly, "All my life." This response rings truer to me with each passing year of ministry. Yet whether we are entering ministry straight out of seminary or have served in pastoral ministry for forty years, we must ask what we can do each week to ready our spirit to teach Scripture from the pulpit.

Prayer as Sermon Preparation

For Augustine, prayer forms the preacher, the study, and the delivery. To preach with a humble and loving spirit, a preacher must prepare the sermon on his knees. A cruciform delivery of the sermon requires a sacrificial life of prayer throughout the week.

Augustine prioritized prayer in sermon preparation—not technical grammatical and contextual exegesis, not coming up with a clear outline, not researching illustrations, not reading books on the subject, not writing out the sermon, not practicing the delivery, but prayer. Prayer is the way to humility and healing. These other aspects of sermon preparation can play a significant role, but prayer exceeds everything else. Prayer humbles the preacher. Prayer fills the preacher with the love of God. Prayer forms the spirit of the preacher. To preach in the spirit of the Scriptures, a preacher must pray the Scriptures.

In *Teaching Christianity* Augustine instructs pastor-teachers on how to understand Scripture and teach it to others. In the final chapter of this handbook on pastoral theology and preaching, Augustine counsels pastors that when they have "good and holy" things to say, they ensure that "listeners understand them, enjoy them, obey them." Augustine explains how the preacher can accomplish these objectives: "It is more the piety of prayer than the ready facility of orators that enables him to do so; by praying then both for himself and for those he is about to address, let him be a pray-er before being a speaker. At the very moment he steps up to speak, before he even opens his mouth and says a word, let him lift up his thirsty soul to God, begging that it may belch forth what it has quaffed, or pour out what he has filled it with."[39]

"Let him be a pray-er before being a speaker." Before reading for the sermon, before writing out the sermon, before practicing the sermon, and before

39. Augustine, *Teaching Christianity* 4.15.32.

delivering the sermon, the pastor must prepare by praying for himself and his congregation. Michael Pasquarello relates Augustine's advice to the person of the preacher, summarizing Augustine's teaching on prayer and preaching: "When it's all said and done, a pastor must be a person who prays, a pray-er who is becoming a living sermon."[40]

To the one who wants to become a living sermon, Dietrich Bonhoeffer recommends praying the Psalms. It's possible that a pastoral lifestyle of praying the Psalms forms preachers and their message more than anything else could. Praying the Psalms orders and directs the affections of the preacher and gives the preacher the grammar for preaching. As we preachers pray the Psalms, Jesus Christ prays in us, with us, and for us, offering us the language to express the range of human longing, joy, hope, torment, pain, fear, hate, loneliness, doubt, trust, and guilt. We are most human, and we share in the human experience most deeply, when we pray the Psalms. Bonhoeffer asks, "How is it possible for a man and Jesus Christ to pray the Psalter together?" He answers, "It is the incarnate Son of God, who has borne every human weakness in his own flesh, who here pours out the heart of all humanity before God and who stands in our place and prays for us. . . . It is really our prayer, but since he knows us better than we know ourselves and since he himself was true man for our sakes, it is also really his prayer, and it can become our prayer only because it was his prayer."[41] The continual practice of praying the Psalms with the congregation and in private devotions warms the heart toward God, moves the mind to theological reflection, and habituates the language of the preacher. "Bonhoeffer doesn't assume prayer as a natural activity but as learned by hearing and speaking God's word."[42]

Imagine the possible ways to integrate prayer into sermon preparation. Sometimes I stand at the pulpit before an empty sanctuary and pray through the text. At other times, I walk throughout the sanctuary while reading the text prayerfully and conversing with God about it. On occasion I will lay before the large cross in the chancel and pray through the text. Before preparing a sermon series, we preachers could take a prayer retreat to spend time fasting and praying over the texts in the lectionary or over a book of the Bible we intend to exposit. Before completing the week's sermon preparation, we could consider praying through the church directory, reminding ourselves of who will be receiving our message. We could pray through the church's prayer list to open our mind and heart to the concerns of our listeners. We could pray

40. Pasquarello, "Preaching Life."
41. Bonhoeffer, *Psalms*, 20–21.
42. Pasquarello, "Preaching Life."

through every verse of the sermon text, connecting themes of the passage to the congregation we shepherd. One seasoned minister shared with me how, after preparing the content of his sermon, he would "walk" his sermon. That is, he would take a prayer walk, reflecting on the content and delivery of the message. Whatever prayer practices we implement in our sermon preparation, we must be a pray-er before we are a preacher.

The Bible and the Cure of Souls

Preaching therapeutically with the right spirit requires an ever-growing, prayerful knowledge of Scripture.

In 391, shortly after Valerius, the bishop of Hippo, ordained Augustine to the priesthood, Augustine expressed passionately to him in a letter that he felt ill prepared for the severity of his ministry. He explained to Valerius that "those tears that some of the brothers noticed that I shed in the city at the time of my ordination" were due to his lack of serious study and prayerful reflection on the Scriptures.[43] Augustine literally begged Valerius for a period to study the Scriptures: "I ought to examine carefully all the remedies of [the Lord's] scriptures and, by praying and reading, work that he may grant my soul health suited for such dangerous tasks. I did not do this before because I did not have the time. For I was ordained at the time when we were planning a period of retreat for gaining knowledge of the divine scriptures and wanted to arrange our affairs in order that we could have the leisure for this task."[44]

Augustine explains that he has enough knowledge of the faith for his own salvation but asks, "But how am I to exercise this ministry for the salvation of others, *not seeking what is beneficial for me, but for many, that they may be saved* (1 Cor 10:33)?"[45] Thus, he requests a short time to immerse himself in Scripture. Augustine looked to the Scriptures for his own healing remedies and preached the Scriptures to bring health to his congregation.

Obviously, Augustine did not spend only a short time thinking his way through Scripture and praying Scripture into the deepest places inside of him; he continued to read the Scriptures in a spiritually transforming and worldview-shaping way. *Confessions* prayerfully reflects on his forty-plus years through the lens of Scripture. The text is so saturated with Scripture that it is often difficult to discern where his words end and where Scripture begins and vice versa. Case in point: The first short paragraph of *Confessions* alludes

43. Augustine, *Letters* 21.2.
44. Augustine, *Letters* 21.3.
45. Augustine, *Letters* 21.4.

to four to six biblical texts. Books 11–22 of *The City of God* (417–26) take the reader through a unified account of the story of Scripture from Genesis to Revelation. Following the cultural critique of the Greco-Roman world in books 1–10, the second part of *The City of God* offers the reader a better (scriptural) story as a way to inhabit the realities of this world in light of the world to come. Throughout *The City of God* Augustine reimagines language and culture through the lens of the biblical narrative. This is a pastoral act. Truly, Augustine took the "pick it up and read, pick it up and read" of his conversion as a lifelong calling.[46]

For therapeutic "Augustinian" preaching, preachers must aim at acquiring a lived knowledge of the main storyline of Scripture, trace out how the Bible is forming their own inner beings, and understand the basics of how the biblical narrative works out in their daily interactions in public spaces. Thus, a therapeutic approach to preaching does more than persuade congregants of the truthfulness of Scripture; it helps them flourish in their daily realities.

Unlike much of today's preaching, Augustine was not atomistic in his approach. While he could do a close reading of the text and pay careful attention to the minute details of a particular passage of Scripture, he would most often keep before himself "the whole counsel of God" (Acts 20:27 ESV), comparing one Scripture with another. He would read a singular text in the light of many other Scriptures. Further, he would preach one text in the context of bigger theological themes. The whole counsel of God includes Christ, our experience of God's presence, and the love of God working in our lives.[47] This is where the personal story of the preacher, the lived story of the congregant, and the big story of Scripture intersect.

Augustine had a method of taking a universal theological truth and applying it directly to his congregation, a method that has a way of ringing true for us today. Bray explains why Augustine succeeded at preaching this way: "One of the main reasons for Augustine's success in this is that he believed that the subject matter for his sermons was given to him from the Bible, which, as God's Word, contained all that was needed for the salvation of his people. Rather than speak directly to what he thought were their immediate needs, he looked for clues in the Scriptures that he could then apply to them."[48] The fallen condition of humankind remains the same, as does the remedy of Christ for the ills of all people. This universal cure is applied through the Scripture to the sicknesses of those in a local congregation. The healing power of Christ

46. Augustine, *Confessions* 8.12.29.
47. Bray, *Augustine on the Christian Life*, 178.
48. Bray, *Augustine on the Christian Life*, 176–77.

received through the preaching of Scripture is first applied to the preacher and then, through the preacher, to the congregation.

Before preaching to others, Augustine preached the Scriptures to himself: "I too make bold to add my own exhortation to you; and while I'm exhorting you, to take a look at myself. After all, it's a futile preacher outwardly of God's word, who isn't also inwardly a listener."[49] Howard Hendricks, my beloved hermeneutics teacher at Dallas Theological Seminary, tells the following anecdote to illustrate the importance of applying the Scriptures to our life: "A man once told me, 'You know, Brother Hendricks, I've been through the Bible twelve times.' But the real question is, how many times has the Bible been through him?"[50] This is especially true for the preacher, as illustrated in Haddon Robinson's classic definition of expository preaching: "Expository preaching is the communication of a biblical concept, derived from and transmitted through a historical, grammatical, and literary study of a passage in its context, *which the Holy Spirit first applies to the personality and experience of the preacher, then through the preacher, applies to the hearers.*"[51]

How do we prepare a biblical sermon that brings healing to our congregation? We prepare it with our whole lives.

The Whole Christ and Preaching

Let's return to the pastor in the introduction to chapter 1. He is overwhelmed, feeling inadequate in light of the complexity of the relational brokenness and spiritual illnesses of his flock. How can he bring a healing word from Scripture for his congregation? Perhaps he can't or, at least, shouldn't put the weight of congregational health on his preaching.

The sermon is just one aspect of a larger matrix in which the congregation can hear God's word. Oliver O'Donovan relieves some of the burden put on the sermon alone: "Reading is continued in a process of interpretative reflection on the text of Scripture, a process that includes every aspect of the Church's teaching, for the Church can teach nothing except on the foundation of reflection on Scripture. It begins, as its originating moment, in preaching, but continues outside the liturgy in other forms of Christian instruction, and, because instruction is *communication*, it continues in the thoughts and reflections of every believer invited to meditate upon the word

49. Augustine, *Sermons* 179.1.
50. Hendricks and Hendricks, *Living by the Book*, 284.
51. Robinson, *Biblical Preaching*, 5 (italics added).

of God."[52] The congregation must do its own work, reflecting on Scripture inside and outside the formal worship service.

But even within the worship service, the pastor does not carry the entire burden of congregational health during the preaching event. Christ is the one preaching in and through the preacher. But more than that, as the whole Christ, Christ preaches throughout the service in the reading of the Psalms, the singing of hymns, the reciting of the Lord's Prayer and the Apostle's Creed, and the reading of other Scriptures. The whole Christ speaks through the sermon in the context of the whole service. The whole Christ carries the whole service and the whole sermon.

According to Augustine, the humble Christ speaks within the congregant and the congregation: "I am speaking about the humility of Christ, my brothers and sisters. . . . To set out or say anything adequate about the humility of Christ, I am not qualified, indeed, I fail completely. I recommend all of it to your meditations, and I will not satisfy you as my listeners. Meditate on the humility of Christ. But who, you ask, will display it to us, if not you? Let him speak within you. The one dwelling within you says it much better than the one shouting from outside."[53]

In the totus Christus, God listens to his own voice through the preacher and in the congregation. "Time and again Augustine returned to this theme, insisting that God only listens to his own voice and trusting that that is what God was hearing through the human preacher."[54] Augustine presents this great mystery in his introduction to Psalm 99: "Whatever instrument God's voice employs, God's voice it is still. Nothing but his own voice sounds sweetly in his ears. When we speak we delight him, as long as he speaks through us."[55] That's preaching the word. God speaking in, through, and to his gathered congregation—the whole Christ.

Jesus Christ is the doctor and the teacher. He instructs and heals through the liturgies, the sacraments, and the sermons in the life of the whole Christ. "[Augustine] advises them to continue the 'usual treatment,'—the conversation about the scriptures in the context of the eucharistic liturgy—even if it stings, to cultivate a love for the light, and constantly to entreat the physician to cure them."[56]

The pastor is like an intern who offers the healing medicine under the authority of the doctor. He is like a tutor who offers advice for understanding

52. O'Donovan, "What Kind of Community Is the Church?," 191 (italics original).
53. Augustine, *Homilies on the Gospel of John* 3.15.
54. Bray, *Augustine on the Christian Life*, 175–76.
55. Augustine, *Expositions of the Psalms* 99.1.
56. Kolbet, *Augustine and the Cure of Souls*, 191.

the instruction of the master teacher. "[Augustine] was their teacher only as a subordinate and, with the people, a fellow student of Christ. The bishop teaching from his *cathedra* was not the true master, whose seat was in heaven; he was more like an older student who could offer advice and tutoring to the others in the class."[57]

Finally, yes, the church is a hospital, but it is also a classroom where Christ instructs his students through the sacraments and the preaching.

> Augustine as preacher and bishop presents [the] sacrament of the humble Word in his preaching, establishing the school of Christ on earth who listens to Christ in heaven. In the liturgy, the Church receives a foretaste of the eschatological goal to which the Christian life, and Augustine's sermons, are directed. The One Word unifies the church through the sacrament of his humility.
>
> All those gathered by grace to receive this sacrament become participators in the *totus Christus*, the whole Christ, and so become unified. This is a critical doctrine which pervades all of Augustine's preaching. The *totus Christus*, as a sacramental doctrine, takes the *sacramentum* of the body gathered hearing the preaching of the Word as a sign of the *res*, the reality, which is the exalted Christ, body and head. When the word is preached, all partake of the *sacramentum* which points to the eschatological reality of the resurrection.[58]

Like the Eucharist, which is a "visible word," preaching is an "audible" sacrament of healing: the whole Christ healing the whole person through the humble preaching of the whole text of Scripture.[59]

Conclusion

Christ brings the healing that we humans most truly desire. He heals our infirmities by restoring us to true happiness and returning us to our truest selves: lovers of God and neighbor. Let us end with a part of Augustine's conclusion to sermon 117, as a sort of case study of this topic that weaves together so many of the themes we have discussed in this chapter. I ask you to quiet your minds and allow the bishop's words to give rest to your pastoral soul:

> What does he say himself, after all, to the weak and infirm, so that they may recover that kind of sight and to some extent at least attain to or brush against the Word through which all things were made? *Come to me, all you who toil*

57. Burns, *Augustine's Preached Theology*, 180.
58. Kim, *Way of Humility*, 140–41.
59. Cameron, introduction, 28–29.

and are overburdened, and I will refresh you. Take my yoke upon you and learn of me; because I am meek and humble of heart (Mt 11:28–29). What is this harangue that the master, the Son of God, the Wisdom of God through whom all things were made, is addressing to us? He is calling the human race, and saying, *Come to me, all you who toil, and learn of me*. You were thinking, no doubt, that the Wisdom of God was going to say, "Learn how I made the heavens and the stars; also, since in me all things, even before they were made, had been numbered how in virtue of their unchangeable ideas even the hairs of your head have been numbered." Is that the sort of thing you were thinking she would say? No; but first this: "*that I am meek and humble of heart*."

There is what you have got to get hold of, brothers and sisters, and it's certainly little enough. We are striving for great things; let us lay hold of little things, and we shall be great. Do you wish to lay hold of the loftiness of God? First catch hold of God's lowliness. Deign to be lowly, to be humble, because God has deigned to be lowly and humble on the same account, yours, not his own. So catch hold of Christ's humility, learn to be humble, don't be proud. Confess your infirmity, lie there patiently in the presence of the doctor. When you have caught hold of his humility, you start rising up with him. Not as though he has to rise, insofar as he is the Word; but it's you, rather, who do so, so that he may be grasped by you more and more.[60]

60. Augustine, *Sermons* 117.17 (italics original).

PART THREE

The Whole Story

FIVE

Fortifying the Fragilized

We are now living in a spiritual super-nova, a kind of galloping pluralism on the spiritual plane.

—Charles Taylor, *A Secular Age*

We're all Thomas now.

—James K. A. Smith, *How (Not) to Be Secular*

The scriptures are a providentially ordered resource for the shaping and reformation of the Christian's imagination and desire. The reformation of imagination and desire is a reformation of the human soul—the soul that finds its mission and true end as *imago Dei* within the body of Christ.

—Lewis Ayres, "The Soul and the Reading of Scripture"

Some may imagine that one as towering as Augustine, who wielded the ecclesial power of a bishop, would have preached the word of God with thunderous and authoritative pronouncements. But this was not the case. Augustine gently and patiently persuaded his listeners to the wisdom and healing power of

---

Portions of the material in this chapter—sometimes in a slightly modified form—originally appeared in Mark Allen, "The City of God and the City of Man," *Faith and the Academy* 6, no. 1 (Fall 2021): 8–11; and Joshua D. Chatraw and Mark D. Allen, *The Augustine Way: Retrieving a Vision for the Church's Apologetic Witness* (Baker Academic, 2023). These materials are used by permission.

Scripture's witness to Jesus Christ. The culture of his day, though framed with Christian governmental structures built through the leadership of emperors such as Constantine and Theodosius, remained deeply pluralistic. Deeper forces embedded in the culture through hundreds of years of pagan influence resisted Christianity's hold on the levers of power. Augustine preached to people wading daily in the crosscurrents of Christianity and pagan pluralism.

Recently, during the last century, more of Augustine's sermons and letters were discovered, and Peter Brown finds that the Augustine of these sermons and letters seems "to be considerably less the authoritarian, stern figure that my reading of the evidence available to me in the 1960s had led me to suspect."[1] Therefore, Brown offers a fresh description of Augustine's ministry context: "Paganism, although officially suppressed by Imperial laws and frequently declared by triumphant Christian writers to be virtually non-existent, had by no means given way to Christianity in the cities of Roman North Africa. . . . The medieval Christendom to which Augustine's thought contributed so heavily was still a long way away from the North Africa of Augustine. . . . This new picture of Augustine the bishop [reveals him] at work in a more fluid environment than we had thought."[2]

Triumphant Christian claims may have denied paganism's vitality in the cities of North Africa, but the facts on the ground reveal that paganism was alive and well, even within Augustine's flock. On at least one occasion he felt compelled to abandon his proposed sermon topic because of the unyielding obstinacy of the crowd.[3]

Brown states that Augustine's sermons were not authoritarian, ex cathedra declarations but more like "dialogues with the crowd." We see in them Augustine pastorally and patiently persuading the unconvinced. "One senses in them the constant presence of the unpersuaded, the indifferent and the downright disobedient."[4]

Thus, Augustine became a pastor-apologist who embraced the need to persuade others—whether Christian or pagan—to have faith and persevere in the wisdom and healing of Jesus Christ. Whether evangelizing or discipling, Augustine found it necessary to defend the Christian faith and persuade others to its beauty, goodness, and truth.

Today in Western society Christianity has lost its taken-for-granted status. Faith has been fragilized.[5] Pluralism has run amok. Alternative options to

1. Brown, *Augustine of Hippo*, 445.
2. Brown, *Augustine of Hippo*, 447.
3. Brown, *Augustine of Hippo*, 447.
4. Brown, *Augustine of Hippo*, 446.
5. Taylor, *Secular Age*, 303–4, 437, 531–32, 556, 595.

Christianity multiply more rapidly than we can classify them. To do the work of an evangelist and make disciples today, the pastor must be a persuader, a vigilant apologist for the Christian faith.

I hear some of you objecting. "That's not me. I'm a pastor, not an apologist." I get that. In fact, I voiced some of the same feelings in *Apologetics at the Cross*:

> The apologists who helped me most had an incredible ability to think quickly on their feet, to draw instantly from an impeccable memory and a vast storehouse of knowledge, and to spot a logical fallacy in a split second. They did it all with complete calm and almost no emotion, Spock-like. As a pastor, whenever I preached on proofs of the resurrection or led a small group on defending the Christian faith, I felt like I was wearing an ill-fitting suit, trying to be someone I was not. My greatest fear was that someone would ask a question beyond what I had studied and I would look like—well, what I would look like if I were ever a contestant on the game show *Jeopardy*. It seemed that apologetics required me to speak from the brain more than the heart.[6]

When I write of persuasion and apologetics, I am referring to a different way of defending the faith: an Augustinian apologetic that considers the whole person and their cultural situatedness. This may be different from the approaches to persuasion and apologetics that you have been exposed to. Augustine's view of integrated personhood and cultural embodiment shaped the way he persuaded others to come to the faith, remain in the faith, and grow in the faith.

After the sack of Rome, Roman traditionalists accused Christianity of causing Rome's fall. Many probing questions about the relationship between Christianity and the empire arose at the time, but the inquiry that most stubbornly occupied Augustine was sent to him in a letter, around 411 or 412, from a friend and an imperial official named Marcellinus. Marcellinus noted a very specific objection from an "illustrious lord" named Volusian. In Marcellinus's own words, the following is Volusian's objection to Christianity's relevance and practicality in the public square: "Moreover, the preaching and teaching of Christ is in no way compatible with the practices of the state, since, as many say, it is clear that it is his commandment that we should repay no one with evil for evil, that we should offer the other cheek to one who strikes us, give our coat to one who insists on taking our cloak, and go twice the distance with someone who wants to force us to go with him."[7] For Volusian, Christianity

6. Chatraw and Allen, *Apologetics at the Cross*, 20.
7. Augustine, *Letters* 136.2.

simply could not work in the real world. The kind of Christian virtue expressed in the Sermon on the Mount was wholly impractical.

Augustine developed a pastoral and persuasive response, a thoughtful defense of the Christian faith more than a decade in the making—*The City of God*. He referred to it as "a massive work, and arduous," and regarded it as a promise kept and a debt paid to his friend Marcellinus, who was falsely accused of a crime and tragically executed in 413. In writing *The City of God* for his beloved Marcellinus, Augustine asserted that he took up the primary "task of defending the most glorious city of God." In the preface to *The City of God*, he states his purpose: "I have undertaken to defend [the city of God] against those who prefer their own gods to its founder."[8]

With his purpose set, Augustine developed *The City of God* with three kinds of readers in mind. The first were "pagan critics of Christianity and 'these Christian times.'"[9] Such people, eager to blame Christianity for the sack of Rome, never liked the wedding of empire to Christianity in the first place. Rather, they were pagan traditionalists who had long sought a return to the glories of Rome that had existed before Christianity. They blamed Christianity for many of society's ills, vigorously challenged the religion's practicality for the actual world, and doubted that it had any hope of bringing about peace and prosperity. More zealous members of this camp opposed any remnant of vibrant Christianity, arguing that its ethical norms were out of step with broader society, particularly the universal call for people to embrace the claims of the gospel. Such exclusiveness was insufferably narrow, denying people the freedom to worship their own gods and enjoy culturally sanctioned pleasures.

Second, Augustine wrote for "Christians who have, in one degree or another, turned against their faith."[10] In today's terms, we might say they had deconstructed. Under the pressures caused by Christianity's diminishing influence and increasingly fragile place in culture, some were walking away from the faith altogether, convinced it did not belong in the emerging world.

Third, Augustine wrote for "Christians who stand in need of a wider vindication of their belief over against the accumulated weight of the Roman religious and political tradition which represented Christianity as a betrayal of all that had made Rome great and, most especially, as a betrayal of its gods."[11] Even among the faithful, doubt crept in, loosening their confidence in the tenets of their Christian faith.

8. Augustine, *City of God* 1, preface.
9. Babcock, introduction, xiii–xiv.
10. Babcock, introduction, xiv.
11. Babcock, introduction, xiv.

How do we reach the hardened skeptics or honest doubters? How do we disciple those who struggle with the fragilization of their faith? How do we reach out to those who have walked away from the faith?

First, who are those who have walked away from the faith, and why have they departed? Understanding their deconversion or deconstruction will help us lovingly persuade them back to the faith, but also it will aid us in reaching those who have not yet believed and in discipling others so that they do not walk away.

To understand those who are experiencing the malaise of fragilized faith, a few stories may help. Stories are more helpful than statistics.[12] My friend Jack Carson shares accounts of friends who walked away from the faith:

> When I was in high school, Jim was one of the most active members of my youth group. He attended every gathering and was friendly with everyone. Wise, honest, and full of conviction, Jim was the perfect picture of a faithful Christian young man. We lost contact with each other after high school, but I recently reconnected with him through Instagram and learned that he no longer considers himself a Christian. He had, apparently, first experienced doubts while attending our youth group. As far as I know, he never told anyone. Perhaps he was worried about the social stigma; maybe he was tired of hearing the all-too-familiar arguments as if they were enough.
>
> When he went off to college, Jim's seedling doubts grew into something he couldn't ignore. He began identifying as bisexual. In the church environment we grew up in, there wasn't much of a positive sexual vision on offer. Instead, we were taught rules and a certain sensibility: being gay was simply wrong and gross. Little more was said about it. I guess it isn't very surprising that Jim isn't a Christian after more than eight years in that environment. Christianity didn't seem to fit Jim anymore.[13]

Jack Carson also recounts Ashley's deconversion story. She attended a private Christian school. Her parents would not allow her to date, presented her with a purity ring, and enrolled her in a Christian college with the hopes of her finding a good Christian man to marry. Ashley felt that this form of Christianity stifled her emotionally and intellectually, to the point of abuse. She explored other forms of Christianity only to have her faith frustrated. Christian leaders' support of immoral politicians discouraged her faith even further. For Ashley, "Christianity just doesn't seem good anymore."[14]

12. For statistics and analysis of the deconverted and religiously unaffiliated, see Burge, *Nones*.
13. Chatraw and Carson, *Surprised by Doubt*, 4.
14. Chatraw and Carson, *Surprised by Doubt*, 4–5.

Taylor faced a barrage of attacks on the credibility of the Christian faith. YouTube videos and Reddit threads chipped away at her faith. At times, she would find some evidence or rational explanation that would bolster her belief in the reliability of the Christian faith, but then another challenge would come along, undermining her confidence. Maintaining her Christian faith became exhausting. "Taylor has given up on trying to banish the doubts that have plagued her for so long. She has deconverted."[15]

These stories are all too familiar. And if we are honest, they hit a little too close to home. How do we keep members of our congregation and ourselves from walking away from the faith due to the weight of social pressures and personal doubts? Is there a way to bring back those who have turned against their original faith? How do we make disciples who will not give way to the intellectual and moral forces of our late modern world? How do we do evangelism in a skeptical age? There is no silver-bullet answer to these questions. But there is an Augustinian way that can help us bring secularized people into the fold, shepherd sheep who are prone to wander, and keep the flock feeding together in rich, green pastures.

James K. A. Smith describes these days as a time in which "believing doesn't come easy. Faith is fraught; confession is haunted by an inescapable sense of its contestability. We don't believe instead of doubting; we believe *while* doubting."[16]

Again, I am not offering you the "key" to persuading those who have a hard time believing, to turning back those who have walked away, or to keeping in those who are considering opting out. But Augustine has given us a way to minister to these three groups.

Basically, to defend the faith against skepticism and to persuade some to remain in the faith and others to return to the faith, Augustine tells us his own story. As an older and wiser pastor, he recounts for those of his flock his own spiritual journey. He does this in one long prayer in *Confessions*. *Confessions* predates *The City of God*. It serves as a kind of prequel, a more personal apologetic that prepares him to write his mammoth cultural apologetic. Before a pastor attempts to persuade the larger world, they must take their own personal journey. Augustine discovered that his intellectual journey could not be separated from his spiritual quest, and he shared his spiritual path with other travelers under his spiritual care.

When meeting with individuals, ministering in small groups, and developing evangelistic and discipling ministries, consider the following Augustinian

15. Chatraw and Carson, *Surprised by Doubt*, 5.

16. J. K. A. Smith, *How (Not) to Be Secular*, 4 (italics original).

questions: What story are you living in? What are you seeking? What authority are you living under? And what community is forming you?

What Story Are You Living In?

Alasdair MacIntyre has famously written, "I can only answer the question 'What am I to do?' if I can answer the prior question 'Of what story or stories do I find myself a part?'"[17] Everyone lives in some kind of story, whether they are aware of it or not. Scholars refer to this "story" in different ways: worldview, cultural embeddedness, social imaginary, and so on. These stories can be personal, local, regional, national, or international. As pastors we can help those who are having doubts and those who have deconverted develop a higher level of self-awareness and critique the stories they are living in.

For example, a contemporary story that undermines Christian confidence is the coming-of-age narrative. This social imaginary may sound something like this: "We have matured beyond the naivete of Christianity. We believe in the facts. In science we trust. Christianity is for the weak—those who need a crutch and are afraid to face the cold, hard truth. Yes, we are spiritual, but we reject the hypocrisy of institutional religion. Christian myths must be left behind as we press forward on our honest quest for truth. We choose hard rationality, intellectual inquiry, scientific discovery, and cultural progress over narrow, backward-looking religion."

The coming-of-age story is nothing new; it's at least as ancient as the fourth century. In *Confessions*, Augustine recounts his own coming-of-age narrative. He left the "backwoods" Christianity of his mother in Thagaste, North Africa, and set out on an ambitious quest for success and certainty among the cultural elites of his day. He left behind what he perceived at the time to be Scripture's crudeness and immaturity as compared to the dignified prose of the likes of Cicero. He joined the Manichaeans, the religious rationalists of his day, where he met other young "brights" who strode with the intellectual swagger of today's New Atheists. At that time Augustine had discovered a more rational, moral, and spiritual way of being in the world—at least, he thought he had.

After nine years with this group, he became disenchanted with them. The Manichaeans did not have all the answers. The absolute, rational certainty that Augustine had hoped to discover in them came short of his expectations. Further, they did not have the spiritual resources to satisfy his restless quest. What had felt like an *intellectual* journey turned out to be primarily

17. MacIntyre, *After Virtue*, 216.

a soul quest for something else. His coming-of-age story turned out to be a subtraction story. He had deleted aspects of Christianity from his story but hadn't actually added anything substantial or positive to his life's journey. Yes, he had felt the euphoria of leaving behind his old faith, but ultimately he discovered that his quest had led him nowhere.

As his story goes on, we see that Augustine's restless heart found rest in God, and the story and stories of Scripture became the narrative framework of his spiritual journey. Significantly, the deeper structure of Augustine's spiritual autobiography in *Confessions* is the story of the prodigal son. Further, we hear echoes of other scriptural stories throughout the work. For example, the story of Eden provides the narrative framework for his famous "pear story."[18] If you pick up a copy of *Confessions* with scriptural footnotes that indicate his quotes or allusions to scriptural texts, you will likely be amazed at how Scripture's story has become Augustine's story. He speaks in the language of Scripture.

Augustine became aware of the story he was living in. He consciously turned to the scriptural story, a story that has Christ the mediator, healer, and teacher at its center. To disciple Christians who had been shaken by doubts and to help those who had deconstructed return, he had to first understand the stories that shaped him and the redemptive story he was living in. This self-awareness prepared him to make others aware of the insufficiency of alternative stories and the potential for flourishing in Scripture's redemptive story. A whole-life pastor must take this personal journey from false narratives to the true story to help others answer the question "What story am I living in?"

Reflecting on our cultural moment and considering life on the ground at the local church where I pastor, I can quickly come up with a list of themes from stories people are living in today:

- self-discovery, self-actualization, and self-care
- inclusion
- finding a soulmate
- raising healthy and successful children
- professional success
- academic accomplishment
- making beautiful things, like gardens, food, art, music, literature, homes
- sex

18. Augustine, *Confessions* 2.4.9.

- pleasure
- leisure
- sports
- exercise
- style, beauty, and appearances
- religion
- philanthropy
- justice
- power, control, and domination

The list could go on. Most of us live at the intersection of many of these stories, though one theme often dominates. These themes are not all bad. In many ways, they can be a part of living and telling a better story, one that follows the narrative of Scripture and is grounded in the redemptive story of Jesus, our teacher and healer. But these stories are not meant to carry the weight of our lives. They cannot provide the deeper structure and lasting flourishing of our existence.

In *Telling a Better Story: How to Talk About God in a Skeptical Age*, Josh Chatraw helps us imagine a better meaning, a better true self, a better happiness, a better inclusiveness, and a better reason. The Christian story can capture the other narratives and redeem the best aspects of each. Chatraw writes, "The good news is that we don't have to muster up our own story. We've been given a story that is more than just true; it is the *best story ever told*. It is the story that makes sense of all other stories humans tell about the world."[19]

Our efforts to produce healthy, well-adjusted children, to succeed at our job, to gain the levers of power, to put an end to poverty, or to create beautiful things cannot bear the weight of our lives. But the whole story of God can. What happens when youthful beauty fades? When the knees give out? When a financial reversal happens? When we are fired at work or when we are divorced at home? When our children go another way? The redemptive story of Jesus Christ as revealed in Scripture can bear the weight of these losses and disappointments. It's an everlasting story. As pastors we help people identify and critique the stories they live in and lead them to live in the best story, a holistic narrative that makes sense out of all other stories. Taking us on a hopeful journey to heavenly happiness, Augustine offers us an integrated story that has Jesus Christ at the center as our teacher and healer.

19. Chatraw, *Telling a Better Story*, 50 (italics original).

What Are You Seeking?

Augustine famously frames *Confessions* as a spiritual quest. The book opens with the claim that "our heart is unquiet until it rests in you":

> Great are you, O Lord, and exceedingly worthy of praise; your power is immense, and your wisdom beyond reckoning. And so we humans, who are a due part of your creation, long to praise you—we who carry our mortality about with us, carry the evidence of our sin and with it the proof that you thwart the proud. Yet these humans, due part of your creation as they are, still do long to praise you. You stir us so that praising you may bring us joy, because you have made us and drawn us to yourself, and our heart is unquiet until it rests in you.[20]

Our heart is unquiet, or restless, until it finds rest in God. *Confessions* begins with a quest, one that is led along by new and fresh questions. It is a book about seeking from start to finish, about a quest driven along by questions. In the very next paragraph, Augustine begins to raise questions:

> Grant me to know and understand, Lord, which comes first: to call upon you or to praise you? To know you or to call upon you? Must we know you before we can call upon you? Anyone who invokes what is still unknown may be making a mistake. Or should you be invoked first, so that we may then come to know you? But how can people call upon someone in whom they do not yet believe? And how can they believe without a preacher? But scripture tells us that those who seek the Lord will praise him, for as they seek they find him, and on finding him they will praise him. Let me seek you, then, Lord, even while I am calling upon you, and call upon you even as I believe in you; for to us you have indeed been preached. My faith calls upon you, Lord, this faith which is your gift to me, which you have breathed into me through the humanity of your Son and the ministry of your preacher.[21]

The entire book is driven along by questions. It is a story of a seeker.

This process of seeking continues until Augustine concludes his restless quest with the reality check that the fullness of rest will not be achieved until "we too may rest in you, in the Sabbath of eternal life."[22] For some, this might sound discouraging; we will never be fully at rest until the repose of the next life. Contrariwise, this is actually a hopeful orienting point, reminding the *quest*ioner that the journey is not pointless. Learning to ask the right questions

20. Augustine, *Confessions* 1.1.
21. Augustine, *Confessions* 1.1.
22. Augustine, *Confessions* 13.36.51.

can lead one toward home, toward eternal rest in God—each person's true north.

The final few paragraphs of *Confessions* are not a conclusion, as we might expect. Actually, the final sentences of the book situate us in a future-oriented life of searching, longing, and being: "Let us rather ask of you [God], seek in you, knock at your door. Only so will we receive, only so find, and only so will the door be opened to us."[23] That is, as lovers seeking understanding, we continue our quest for God with open-ended expectation. Charles T. Mathewes notes the somewhat odd final word of the book: "*aperietur*, 'will be' or 'shall be opened.'"[24] This "conclusion" has an awareness that the ultimate resolution to the questioning search will not be fully realized until we rest in eternal repose in God, until we receive the true wisdom we were made for and we long for.[25]

Humans are lovers, lovers of God and lovers of neighbor in God. We are worshipers. And we are on a journey to the eternal presence of God, the one we were made for, in order to live the way we were meant to live.

But our loves are disordered. We are twisted and bent toward other loves. We worship idols. The false stories that we live in form us and aim our wills toward the wrong telos. Alternative ways of being in the world bend our hearts toward false gods like money, sex, and power. Even good things can be made into false gods/idols. We make things that are penultimate, ultimate. According to Augustine, the goods of this world are to be used to bring us to God and to shape us toward loving God and showing charity to others. Marriage, children, a friend, food, social justice, sports, politics, and so on—all good in their proper place—can become an end in themselves, sucking up our energy and diverting our focus from what is best: love of God and love of neighbor in the love of God. We are seekers, pursuing what gives us meaning and what satisfies our desires. Yet false gods will turn on us. They will disappoint us every time, leaving us empty—until we move on to the next thing to begin this cycle over again.

In our evangelism and discipleship ministries, we must be convinced in our own hearts that people have been made to worship the true God, and we must appeal to their best and truest desire to love God and to share his love with others. They are most fully human when they are laying down their lives for God and serving others. Yes, their flesh—that is, their false, twisted

23. Augustine, *Confessions* 13.38.53. This observation is made in Mathewes, "Liberation of Questioning."

24. Mathewes, "Liberation of Questioning," 539.

25. The above two paragraphs were adapted with permission from Chatraw and Allen, *Augustine Way*, 84–85.

self—will resist, but we must continue to call them forth to the mediator who will reorder their loves, teach them the way to live, and heal their fragmented hearts. Jesus will gather the scattered fragments of their lives and reorder and redirect them into an integrated life focused on the God they will encounter at the end of their hopeful journey.

Augustine expresses his own darkness and desire for God in *Confessions*:

> O Truth, illumination of my heart,
> let not my own darkness speak to me!
> I slid away to material things, sank into shadow,
> yet even there, even from there, I loved you.
> Away I wandered, yet I remembered you.
> I heard your voice behind me, calling me back,
> yet scarcely heard it for the tumult of the unquiet.
> See now, I come back to you,
> fevered and panting for your fountain.
> Let no one bar my way,
> let me drink it and draw life from it.
> Let me not be my own life:
> evil was the life I lived of myself;
> I was death to me; but in you I begin to live again.
> Speak to me yourself, converse with me.
> I have believed your scriptures,
> but those words are full of hidden meaning.[26]

Augustine knows that his dark heart only leads to a life in the shadows, a restless, tumultuous life. Yet he pants for God. He longs for God, the fountain of all that is really life.

In my teaching I have begun to ask the questions "Do you know why people go to church? Do you know what people really want out of church?" The answer to both, quite simply, is God. Not programs for their kids. Not philanthropic ministries. Not self-help. Not friends. Not a soulmate. Not social standing. Not cool music. These things are on offer outside of the church. But the church offers God through the preaching of the crucified Savior. The Scriptures, the liturgies, the fellowship, and the mission offer to the seeking hearts what they are truly longing for: God the Father, God the Son, and God the Holy Spirit.

Recall why you got into the ministry. Think about why you are training for ministry. I would dare say that it is not because you want to "run" a church. No, you desire to know God. You are seeking to know him. And you want

26. Augustine, *Confessions* 12.10.10.

to lead other people to his love. And the farther you get down the path, the more you hunger to worship him. That's a good thing. As a pastor, you are becoming more human, more yourself, more of what you were meant to be.

When we are making disciples, we are introducing them to practices and liturgies, to truths and insights that will satisfy their longings for God. Keep this question before not just those you are evangelizing but those you are discipling and wooing back to the faith: "What are you seeking?" Recall that the Augustine who stated at the beginning of *Confessions*, "Our heart is unquiet until it rests in you," is the same Augustine who sums up the book in his final paragraph with the following: "What human can empower another human to understand these things? What angel can grant understanding to another angel? What angel to a human? Let us rather ask of you, seek in you, knock at your door. Only so will we receive, only so find, and only so will the door be opened to us. Amen."[27] He was still asking, seeking, and knocking. Thus, always keep this primary question before the congregation: What do you seek? Persuade them toward what they long for. Defend what they were made to love and worship.

What Authority Are You Living Under?

On his journey away from the Christian faith, Augustine had hoped to find a silver-bullet argument, a syllogism, or a type of rational argument as sure as a mathematical equation, like three plus seven equals ten.[28] He was looking for certainty that could be secured through universal rationality. He had hoped to find this certainty in Manichaeanism. Disappointed, he looked elsewhere. In *Confessions* he records in rapid literary pace his journey from the "defensible" and "intellectually respectable" claims of the Catholic Christian faith to the lack of "definite proofs" of the Manichaeans, to the "more probable views" of various philosophers, to the "doubting everything and wavering" of the Academics.[29] In this intellectual search, Augustine realized that his pursuit was more than intellectual. His quest was for far more than a logical explanation or an answer to a rational question. He longed for spiritual healing from his disoriented, disintegrated wretchedness: "I flatly refused to entrust the cure of my soul's sickness to philosophers who were strangers to the saving name of Christ."[30] The search for healing drove his intellectual quest.

27. Augustine, *Confessions* 13.38.53.
28. Augustine, *Confessions* 6.4.6.
29. Augustine, *Confessions* 5.14.24–25.
30. Augustine, *Confessions* 4.14.25.

Frustrated with his failure to find a universally airtight argument, Augustine returned to the Catholic faith of his parents, although he was not yet convinced of its truth: "I resolved therefore to live as a catechumen in the Catholic Church, which was what my parents had wished for me, until some kind of certainty dawned by which I might direct my steps aright."[31] We may say today that he decided to "try on" Christianity, to see if he could discover a fittedness to it. Would it bring healing? Would it make sense out of his life? Would it provide what he was looking for? Would there be a logical and livable consistency to it?

Most likely reflecting on Augustine's decision to try on the faith of the church, Pascal advises the seeker, "You want to find faith and you do not know the road. You want to be cured of unbelief and you ask for the remedy: learn from those who were once bound like you and who now wager all they have. These are people who know the road you wish to follow, who have been cured of the affliction of which you wish to be cured: follow the way by which they began."[32] Pascal, following Augustine, invites seekers to place themselves on a road traveled by others, to check into a hospital where others are finding healing, to try on the Christian faith, to make an informed and reasonable decision to "sit" in the faith of the church until some kind of certainty dawns on them.

In this journey, Augustine discovered that everyone trusts in some authority. There is no simple, universal rationality obvious to anyone who will simply open their mind. The Manichaeans promised proof and unqualified certainty, but Augustine concluded they were not being honest with themselves or with others. He surmised that everyone believes in something. Faith in something seeks understanding of that something. Everyone lives this way. Choosing the best authority to live under is key. In truth, Augustine found the Catholic Church to be more honest because it admitted mystery, whereas the Manichaeans overreached in their promise to solve the mysteries of the universe through science and reason. Augustine explains, "I came to see that in commanding that certain things must be believed without demonstration the Church was a good deal more moderate and very much less deceitful than those parties who rashly promised knowledge and derided credulity, but then went on to demand belief in a whole host of fabulous and absurd myths which certainly could not be demonstrated."[33] Rather than explain things, the Manichaeans ignored holes in their logic and suppressed honest questions.

31. Augustine, *Confessions* 4.14.25.
32. Pascal, *Pensées* (trans. Krailsheimer), 119.
33. Augustine, *Confessions* 6.5.7.

What authority are you living under? This is a relevant guiding question to shape our discipleship ministry. We sometimes hear children say, "You're not the boss of me." They may follow up with, or at least imply, "I'm the boss of me." We live in a "You're not the boss of me; I'm the boss of me" generation. That's not all bad. It's good to have personal agency, to know our identity, to live within and out of the authentic self that we are.[34] But we have taken the freedom to express ourselves, to live our truth, to be whoever and whatever we want, to an extreme—a soul-shrinking and soul-crushing extreme—that has alienated us from one another, has divided us into tribes, and has left us lonely, anxious, and depressed. We need a better boss than our own selves. We need to try on a better authority, one that will bring the healing we seek, a sovereign who leads us on a path toward happiness and flourishing.

Everyone trusts in an authority. Everyone must believe in witnesses. Our own thoughts and our own eyes are insufficient to determine what is true. Augustine describes his journey to this conclusion:

> So it was, Lord, that you began little by little to work on my heart with your most gentle and merciful hand, and dispose it to reflect how innumerable were the things I believed and held to be true, though I had neither seen them nor been present when they happened. How many truths there were of this kind, such as events of world history, or facts about places and cities I had never seen; how many were the statements I believed on the testimony of friends, or physicians, or various other people; and, indeed, unless we did believe them we should be unable to do anything in this life.[35]

What are we putting our trust in? Who or what is our authority? Augustine concluded that we need sacred Scripture. The Bible is a better authority: "It was because *we were weak* and unable to find the truth by pure reason that we needed the authority of the sacred scriptures; and so I began to see that you would not have endowed them with such authority among all nations unless you had willed human beings to believe in you and seek you through them."[36] No other book has done more to shape the world than the Bible.

This kind of authority calls us to cultivate and norm our ministries in Scripture. But church ministries are not just Bible-content delivery systems. Scriptural teaching goes beyond just inspirational talk. Application of Scripture requires more than coming up with a list of moral principles. Instead, church ministries lead people to feed on the Scriptures as a source of Jesus

34. Taylor, *Ethics of Authenticity*.
35. Augustine, *Confessions* 6.5.7.
36. Augustine, *Confessions* 6.8 (italics original).

Christ's teaching and healing. We present the Scriptures as the story we live in, the place we encounter the one we are seeking, and the source of wisdom and restoration for our lives. We listen to Scripture to hear the voice of our Savior. This approach begins in the pulpit with preaching the gospel of Jesus Christ from all the Scriptures; as Tim Keller advises, "To show how a text fits into its whole canonical context, then, is to show how it points to Christ and gospel salvation, the big idea of the whole Bible. Every time you expound a Bible text, you are not finished unless you demonstrate how it shows us that we cannot save ourselves and that only Jesus can. That means we must preach Christ from every text, which is the same as saying we must preach the gospel every time and not just settle for general inspiration or moralizing."[37]

The church—the whole Christ—is a community formed by the Scriptures and a community forming believers in the authority of Scripture. This leads us to our fourth question.

What Community Is Forming You?

Again, Augustine resolved "to live as a catechumen in the Catholic Church . . . until some kind of certainty dawned by which [he] might direct [his] steps aright."[38] The church became a place of formation for Augustine and a place where God used him to form others in the faith. We are all being formed by a community we inhabit.

I can boast that when I was in the ninth grade, I played football for the Rainelle Rangers in my hometown of Rainelle, West Virginia. I don't remember all the games we won, but I can recall the game we lost. The White Sulphur Springs Green Devils beat us by a single touchdown. (White Sulphur Springs is the home of the famed Greenbrier hotel.) White Sulphur Springs was a much bigger school than we were. They had more boys try out for football than we had in our whole junior high school. And we would have beat them if we hadn't made several silly mistakes. I lined up offside near the goal line. My friend Tony fumbled the ball running for a wide-open touchdown. Other mistakes were made. What I remember the most about the game is that even though we were manly junior high football players, we bawled our eyes out in the locker room after the loss. There we were in our shoulder pads and cleats, crying like babies. Why? Because in three short years of living in that football community, we had collectively learned to

37. Keller, *Preaching*, 48.
38. Augustine, *Confessions* 5.14.25.

hate defeat and love victory, to mourn deeply a loss and celebrate joyfully a win. Our practices on hot and dewy August mornings in the dirt and grass had formed our football intuitions and desires. Our communal routines had shaped us into Rangers—"mighty, mighty Rangers." (I can still hear the liturgical chant in my mind.)

We are liturgical beings shaped by the practices of our community. Our community forms our loves and our hates. What we celebrate shapes our loves. What we mourn forms our dislikes. We are habituated by the norms of our community. Our community affects our rationality, the way we reason toward certain conclusions. Even at an unconscious, pre-reflective level, our social setting shapes the way we see the world and the way we reason toward our conclusions and opinions. The stories our community tells and the myths we honor make us who we are and form how we see the world—which results in "of course" statements:

- Of course, we can love whomever we want to love.
- Of course, we should be inclusive of everyone (except . . .).
- Of course, there is no God.
- Of course, we can trust science over our feelings.
- Of course, we can trust our own feelings and thoughts over some authority.
- Of course, we want to get rich.
- Of course, we need guns to defend ourselves.
- Of course, we should have a right to choose.
- Of course, we want a shiplap accent wall in our house.
- Of course, we hate the Dallas Cowboys.

Have we reasoned our way to these "of course" statements? Sure we have, to some extent. But our community and habits have shaped our rationality. They have formed our intuitions about what we believe and what we deny. So in discipleship, it is imperative for us to reflect on what community is forming us.

The church community is the whole Christ, where we pray together the Psalms, hear the word of God together, die and live together in our baptism, lay down our lives in charity through taking the bread and cup of our Lord together, sing praises together, make confessions together, recite the Apostles' Creed together, pray the Lord's Prayer together, work for the common good and share our means together, live in fellowship together, and bear witness together to the gospel. We experience the mystical presence of Jesus Christ through his body, the church. This community forms our intuitions, desires, and rationality.

- Of course, Jesus Christ died for our sins and arose.
- Of course, we are made to love God and love our neighbor.
- Of course, we love because God is a Holy Trinity of love: Father, Son, Holy Spirit.
- Of course, we live under the authority of Scripture.
- Of course, the church is a hospital, and the gospel heals us.
- Of course, Jesus Christ will return, and we are happy in hope.
- Of course, marriage is between a man and a woman.
- Of course, we are sinful but are saved by grace.
- Of course, God created the universe.
- Of course, Jesus Christ is king over all creation, and following him leads to human flourishing.

The list could go on and on. The church forms our affections and rationality through spiritual disciplines, liturgies, sacraments, teaching, fellowship, and service. "It is in the formative worship of the church—rehearsing the biblical drama whose *telos* is the eschaton—that we learn both the norms for flourishing *and* how to wait."[39] As such, the church is an apologetic community. For example, it defends belief in the crucifixion and resurrection of Jesus Christ by the way church members live in a cruciform manner together. It makes apologists of the Scriptures through explaining and embodying the redemptive story of the Bible. The church's life together presents evidence to the healing power of Jesus Christ and makes a case for the hopefulness of our journey homeward. Timothy Paul Jones refers to this as "ecclesial apologetics." He explains, "For the ecclesial apologist, the role of the church in apologetics is not merely to provide a context where members learn to defend their faith; the life of the church itself is a key evidence for the truth of the faith." *The community that forms us matters.* "Viewed from the perspective of ecclesial apologetics, the moral framework enacted through the church's life is impossible apart from the truth of the biblical metanarrative, which itself presupposes a particular set of metaphysical realities and epistemological structures."[40]

The answer to the question "What community is forming you?" matters.

39. J. K. A. Smith, *Awaiting the King*, 89 (italics original).
40. Jones, "Ecclesial Apologetics," 140.

Conclusion

To persuade others to remain in the faith and return to the faith, we need to envision evangelistic and discipleship ministries that are structured around four key questions:

- What story are you living in?
- What are you seeking?
- What authority are you living under?
- What community is forming you?

The next chapter introduces an Augustinian diagnostic tool and shows how pastors can use this tool to teach their congregations a way to have more productive apologetic conversations. Thus, chapter 6 picks up where this one leaves off. It focuses on personal apologetic interactions. This will prepare the reader for the final chapter, which focuses on an Augustinian approach to public theology. It shows how Augustine helps pastors equip congregants to live out their faith in public spaces. Thus, the next chapter picks up the theme of apologetics and prepares for a transition to public theology.

SIX

Persuading Skeptics

To be a Christian is not simply to believe a list of propositions but also to experience the world through the lens of a meaningful imaginative vision.

—Justin Ariel Bailey, *Reimagining Apologetics*

What are you seeking? Because if these arguments simply add up to a range of quite arid, abstract propositional possibilities, then they're not grabbing you existentially in the way that they would if you were actually prepared to put your life on the line in terms of practices.

—Sarah Coakley, in "Why Believe in God? Part 1," from PBS's *Closer to Truth*

A couple months before I sat down to write this chapter, a Christian women's organization in the Virginian community where I minister invited another pastor and me to speak at one of their gatherings. We were the first males ever asked to speak at one of their events. They asked us to speak about truth.

The topic seemed rather broad, so we decided to sit down with the leaders of the organization to get more specific. When we met, the other pastor, a colleague of mine in my university's biblical and theological studies department, asked them insightful questions to get at the core of their concerns. He's also a licensed counselor, so I learned a lesson on how to discover the deeper concern when someone presents a surface issue.

Originally, when we were asked to speak on truth, I had the impression that they wanted us to provide for them arguments that could shore up their confidence in the truth of Scripture and would equip them to go out and defend the truth. I was not wrong about this, but through our meeting with the three women, we found that they were concerned about their friends, relatives, children, and grandchildren either walking away from the faith or having no interest in the validity of the Bible or the truth of the gospel. I thought their desire for truth was motivated by a desire for intellectual confidence, but I found they were motivated by their love for those they had relationships with.

We developed a different approach to our presentation with them. If we were to simply give them arguments for the veracity of Scripture or present them with evidence for the resurrection of Jesus Christ, then their skeptical friends could google arguments against the reliability of the Scripture or the reality of the resurrection of our Savior. The women of this organization could then google more arguments for the truthfulness of Scripture and the gospel. Then back and forth they would go.

First, we decided to help them learn to listen to their agnostic and uninterested friends and family and to understand the way their friends' and families' affections and rationality have been shaped by the late modern world—a post-Christian, secular social imaginary. Our friends and family who are indifferent to the truth perceive that they are living in a narrative different from the Christian story that has shaped our faith, love, and hope. They conceive the world differently than we do.

Next, after discussing how to ask better questions, we wanted to show them how the Christian story is a better story. It's a better way to live and a better way to die. Basically, in the limited time we had with them, we decided to teach them a modified Inside Out methodology.[1]

In this chapter, I will present the Inside Out diagnostic framework and show you how to use it to equip a congregation to have better apologetic conversations. This approach will help you defend your faith and make a winsome appeal to the gospel with friends and family who reject the truth of Scripture or who simply do not see how the faith could be true for their lives in the twenty-first century.

How does this relate to Augustine's approach? The basic Inside Out framework goes back to the two main sections of Augustine's *The City of God*. His nine-hundred-page (in English) tome is divided into two main sections: Books 1–10 contain an immanent critique of Christianity's rivals in the Greco-Roman world; books 11–22 narrate the redemptive storyline of Scripture to give a better account of what history means and why humanity was created.

1. See Chatraw and Allen, "Preparing to Engage." More on this below.

Augustine goes inside the culture of his day to show its shortcomings and then goes outside to the better story of Scripture and the church's place in the grand narrative. In the first section, Augustine uses pagan sources with very little reference to the Bible. In the second section, Augustine uses Scripture with very little reference to pagan sources. Throughout the work, Augustine argues for the superiority of the Christian faith. The Christian faith makes better sense out of human experience, leads to human flourishing, and accords with the grain of creation.

Curtis Chang notes that today we are doing ministry amid "epochal challenges." Postmodernity has brought on new challenges as we experience cultural shifts from old, traditional ways to new, uncharted ways. The ground is shifting under us as we move from a Christian to a post-Christian world. Chang notes that Augustine also ministered to the church in a time of epochal change. The barbarians invaded Rome during his lifetime, causing a resurgence of paganism in his North African ministry context. Chang states, "Because the truth is that this is not the first time Christianity has needed to figure out what to say when the Western civilization it is attached to seems to be in danger of dying. Augustine awaits our inquiries." But he warns, "It obviously would be foolish to enlist Augustine's actual arguments in *City of God* to respond to today's 'pagan critics.'" Rather than using Augustine's actual arguments—though some would still be relevant in modified forms—he offers an apologetic strategy with three main components:

1. *Entering* the challenger's story
2. *Retelling* the story
3. *Capturing* that retold tale within the gospel metanarrative[2]

I would like to introduce you to a slightly more detailed structure that will help you employ Augustine's basic framework for apologetic conversations. The following diagnostic questions provide scaffolding for persuading hardened skeptics and honest doubters to the Christian faith in a holistic and integrated way. Josh Chatraw and I have given this structure the label "Inside Out." We first introduced Inside Out in the apologetics textbook *Apologetics at the Cross*. Chatraw—the originator of the Inside Out diagnostic process—developed Inside Out further in his book *Telling a Better Story*.[3]

2. This list and the previous quotations are from Chang, *Engaging Unbelief*, 25–26. Chang also demonstrates how Aquinas used a similar strategy.

3. Chatraw, *Telling a Better Story*, 54–74.

The following chart lays out the Inside Out methodology. First, the apologist enters the skeptic's story to affirm and challenge it. Second, the apologist demonstrates how Christianity tells a better story of reality.

Diagnostic Questions for Apologetic Interactions

Inside:

- What can I affirm, and what will I need to challenge?
- Where does this story lead, and is it internally consistent and livable?

Outside:

- Where do the competing views borrow from the Christian story?
- How does the Christian narrative better address our experiences, observations, and history?[4]

Augustine, the Platonists, and Inside Out

The Inside Out method is in some ways a contemporary articulation of Augustine's mode of engagement with Greco-Roman culture. From his greatest work of apologetics, *The City of God*, I would like to demonstrate briefly how these diagnostic questions can be seen in his interactions with Plato and the Platonists. Here I am summarizing, but more could be written analyzing the structure and application of Augustine's Inside Out approach in *The City of God*.

Inside

What Can I Affirm, and What Will I Need to Challenge?

Augustine affirmed much related to the Platonists' (albeit shadowy) view of God. Here is a single example:

> You proclaim the Father and the Son, whom you call the intellect or mind of the Father, and a third intermediate between these two, by whom we presume that you mean the Holy Spirit, and, as is your custom, you call these three gods. In this regard, even though you are using inaccurate terms, you Platonists have to some extent, as if through some faint and shadowy image, caught sight of what we should strive to attain.[5]

4. This chart has been adapted from Chatraw and Allen, *Apologetics at the Cross*, 216–21.
5. Augustine, *City of God* 10.29.

Yet Augustine challenges their belief:

> But you are not willing to acknowledge the incarnation of the immutable Son of God, by which we are saved and through which we are enabled to arrive at the realities in which we believe and which, in some small measure, we understand. In a fashion, then, you see—if only from a great distance and with clouded vision—the country in which we should abide, but you do not keep to the path that leads to it.[6]

Without a belief in the incarnation of Jesus Christ, the Platonists cut themselves off from the true way to come to know God, the God they see in the great distance with only a clouded vision.

Where Does This Story Lead, and Is It Internally Consistent and Livable?

Apart from the particular grace that is given in Jesus Christ, the Platonists have no way to attain the true knowledge of God that they are seeking. They have a belief in grace but lack the means of grace to attain what they desire. Their view of grace is not workable or livable without the humble incarnation of Jesus Christ:

> You do, however, admit that there is such a thing as grace, for you say that it has been granted only to a few to attain to God by the power of intelligence. You do not say "It pleased only a few" or "Only a few desired" but "It has been granted only to a few." There is no doubt, then, that in saying this you are acknowledging the grace of God, not the sufficiency of man. You even use this term quite openly when, following Plato's opinion, you state that, beyond doubt, man cannot by any means achieve the perfection of wisdom in this life, but that, for those who live according to intellect, everything they lack can be made up after this life by God's providence and grace.[7]

Their desires will lead only to frustration unless they recognize the grace revealed in the incarnate Christ: "If only you had recognized *the grace of God through Jesus Christ our Lord* (Rom 7:25)! If only you had been able to see that his very incarnation, by which he assumed a human soul and body, is the supreme example of grace!"[8]

Unsurprisingly, according to Augustine, the problem with the philosophers is they are too proud. If only they would put their trust in the incarnate Lord

6. Augustine, *City of God* 10.29.
7. Augustine, *City of God* 10.29.
8. Augustine, *City of God* 10.29 (italics original).

instead of in the ability of their own intellect to reason and reflect their way to God: "But it takes humility to accept this truth, and it is only with great difficulty that your stiff neck can be persuaded to submit. . . . Why do you persist in this opinion, trying to make it look as though you have rational grounds for fleeing from the Christian faith, unless it is because . . . Christ is humble and you are proud?"[9]

Their ascent to God is unlivable and unattainable through their intellectual reflections. To attain the true knowledge of God, they must humble themselves and trust in the embodied Lord Jesus Christ.

Augustine identifies the Platonists' hang-up with the incarnation and works within their own conceptual world to undermine their objections and to show how their own categories can lead them to accepting the incarnate Christ. He creates doubt within them to open up space for them to believe in the humble, incarnate Savior and submit to the Christian story of redemption. But like the Lord Jesus Christ, they must humble themselves.

Augustine also turns outside of their conceptual world to Christianity's better story.

Outside

Where Do the Competing Views Borrow from the Christian Story?

Augustine cautiously claims that Plato may have been influenced by or may have borrowed from the Scriptures—specifically, from the identity of the one true deity revealed to Moses:

> There is the fact that Plato says that the philosopher is a lover of God, and nothing in those Sacred Scriptures is expressed more ardently than this. But most of all—and this, more than anything, almost leads me to agree that Plato was not unacquainted with the books of Scripture—there is this fact: when God's words were brought to the saintly Moses by an angel, and Moses asked for the name of the one who had charged him to go and deliver the Hebrew people from Egypt, the answer was *I am who I am, and you shall say to the children of Israel, He who is sent me to you* (Ex 3:14). It is as if, in comparison with the one who truly is, because he is immutable, the things which were created mutable have no real existence at all. This is precisely the view that Plato strongly maintained and rigorously urged, and, as far as I know, it can nowhere be found in the works of those who preceded Plato, except where it is said, *I am who I am, and you shall say to them, He who is sent me to you.*[10]

9. Augustine, *City of God* 10.29.
10. Augustine, *City of God* 8.11 (italics original).

Augustine uses this line of reasoning with humility and only as a part of a larger argument for Christianity. It does not stand alone, and he does not put too much weight on it. But he does open the door to use stronger arguments that demonstrate how a skeptic's way of conceiving the world may have been shaped by the Christian story more than that skeptic may realize.

How Does the Christian Narrative Better Address Our Experiences, Observations, and History?

Augustine closes his argument with a negative assessment of Platonism's pride. He emphasizes that becoming a disciple of the incarnate Christ is the way to healing, but being ashamed to receive the medicine of the gospel's better story only makes the Platonists' disease worse: "But there is a reason why God, the great teacher, seemed worthless to the eyes of the proud—because *the Word became flesh and dwelt among us* (Jn 1:14). It is not enough, then, that these wretched people are sick. They also have to exult in their illness and feel ashamed of the medicine by which they could be healed. But the result is not that they are raised up but rather that they are afflicted all the more grievously by their fall."[11] The Christian story is a better story because it heals.

Chang summarizes Augustine's approach: "Augustine responds to his challengers with a willingness to meet on their turf. He inhabits the pagan worldview with appreciation and sympathy. But he also enters in order to retell the pagan story. . . . Yet Augustine realizes that such retellings are themselves inadequate to fully convince the pagan. The tragic flaw of pride dominates too much of his challengers' terrain, seizes too much of their heart. Their eyes must be lifted to a new land, their heart captivated by a new tale."[12] The Inside Out approach works within the skeptic's story to lead them to a better story, one of wholeness and healing.

An Inside Out Workshop

In apologetic and evangelistic conversations, Inside Out is a structure that can guide the dialogue. It is a noncombative way to raise to a conscious level what story a person is living in, what they are seeking, what authority they are living under, and what community is forming them. It is a framework for transitioning to Christianity to show that the Christian faith answers these four questions in a better way. Yet we should not follow the structure too rigidly, since all these questions are in play throughout the conversation.

11. Augustine, *City of God* 10.29 (italics original).
12. Chang, *Engaging Unbelief*, 82.

When teaching students and congregants how to use the Inside Out framework, I usually walk them through the diagnostic questions one right after the other, reminding and showing them how, in real-life conversations, we usually do not inflexibly take others step-by-step through each question. Instead, we will go back and forth between "inside" issues and "outside" issues. Sometimes we may be able to leap right into showing a conversation partner how Christianity is a better story to live in. Yet at other times, we may, like Augustine, make an immanent critique of their way of imagining the world, followed by a reimagining of their story in the light of the scriptural narrative.

In a university classroom or a church gathering, I teach how to use the Inside Out methodology through presenting a profile of a typical late modern "pagan" and following with a discussion of how each diagnostic question may apply to the person in the profile. Just before writing this chapter, I did this exercise in a university classroom. That was last week. This week, a student got my attention before class and said, "Hey, Dr. Allen, I used the Inside Out method in witnessing this weekend." She proceeded to relate to me how it went. The unbeliever did not become a Christian, but she did open herself up to more conversations, especially since she was surprised to discover that she and the student had many things in common.

In our time of epochal change, pastors can use this Augustinian methodology in their approach to ministry. Also, they can train their church members to apply this approach to their own lives. It will help them to defend the faith with modern pagans who oppose Christianity, to calm others in the church who are beginning to experience their own disorienting doubts, and to retrieve those who have wandered from the Christian faith.

I would like to take you through such a workshop. The following example represents one type of story. There are many reasons why different individuals have left the faith or have never believed in the first place. Each pastor will need to adapt their instruction to their ministry context.

This is Gus's story.

> My name is Gus. I grew up in Northern Indiana, where I attended an independent Bible church. From preschool through elementary school, I participated in Awana clubs. (I still remember that "approved workmen are not ashamed.") I learned the Bible verses, earned the patches, and played the games. In the sixth grade, I accepted Christ as my personal savior and was baptized by immersion. In high school, I discovered girls, played sports, and volunteered as a student leader in Young Life.
>
> After graduating first in my class, I went to Purdue University and majored in engineering. In college, I began to question my faith because the Bible, especially the creation story but also many other contradictions, seemed unscientific and

illogical. Also the sexual and financial abuses in the church began to unnerve me. Many of my non-Christian classmates—the "sinners" that I had been warned about—did not actually have devil's horns. Rather, on a secular university campus, I discovered many good and kind people who kept the golden rule better than some Christians I knew. These folks helped me through the sudden and tragic death of my dad, who was killed by a drunk driver. Disappointment with the God of my childhood overwhelmed me. I let go of my last hope in Christianity.

I didn't stop being spiritual. I still respect much of the teaching of Jesus Christ; I just wish more Christians would follow his way. I must admit that institutional religion works for some people, but not for me. A friend once called me a "none." It's true that I have no religious affiliation, but I still have a sense of awe when I am out in nature, like there is something bigger than me and beyond what I can see out there.

I can't say what is right for other people; they should be free to follow their own path. Personally, I look inside myself to my own sense of right and wrong and my own desires to decide what is true for me. Sometimes that seems like the only thing that I know is real.

After college, I picked up an MBA at the University of Michigan and now work as a civil engineer. Someday I hope to become an executive in a large engineering firm. I am trying meditation, and I enjoy the benefits of working out. I'm living with someone I met at the gym. She's funny, intelligent, and caring. In our spare time, we like to hike, bike, ski, and kayak.

I am not certain what happens after we die. I'm not sure we can ever really know anything for certain, but my life is not without purpose. I feel that we discover our own meaning through doing good things for others, contributing at work, and building a few significant relationships.

Yes, I've moved on from Christianity, and now I feel that I am a more authentic and happier person. I have experienced much personal growth by facing the raw difficulties in this world and embracing the glimpses of the wonderful beauties of life. I have my whole life ahead of me, and I am free to make it anything—admittedly, within some limits—I want it to be.[13]

Not every secular person in our communities will fit this profile. Oftentimes we have the most influence with the marginalized and broken. Many of the folks who are open to the gospel are people who have lost everything or have come to the end of themselves. I once witnessed for Christ at the bedside of a friend's mother who was dying of cancer. She and her husband had lived their lives as atheists. When I entered her bedroom, she looked up at me and said, "I am so lost." I shared with her that Jesus came to seek and save the lost and showed her that Jesus is the way, the truth, and the life. She believed

13. Gus is a fictional character, a composite of many individuals who leave the Christian faith in our secular age.

in Jesus Christ that day. Her health rallied, and she began to attend church. Later the cancer took over her body. I visited her once again and asked about her faith in Jesus. She responded, "I love him more now than I did then." She believed until the end.

With this story, I am making two points. One, obviously not everyone will match Gus's profile. Two, even Gus may have a moment when his heart opens back up to the gospel.

I designed this profile because most people know someone like Gus or could imagine a person who has walked Gus's path away from the Christian faith. His profile works well to demonstrate how the Inside Out methodology works. Imagine introducing this profile in a teaching session at your church (or making up your own profile that matches better with the folks in your community) and then taking a group of church members through the Inside Out diagnostic questions to equip them to defend the faith and make a persuasive appeal for the gospel.

Below, I take you through the Inside Out framework. The bullet points give some answers I would give to these questions. Along the way through this section, imagine the answers that your congregants may give. Reflect on how you would coach them through the Inside Out diagnostic tool. Some of the bullet points may represent answers given by your congregants to each diagnostic question.

Inside

What Can I Affirm?

It's important to listen empathically. We must attempt to hear and understand each person genuinely. We must honestly want to connect with their humanity—their disappointments, questions, and desires. We are not listening simply to make our point or to gain their confidence so that we can get a hearing. We sincerely care about their flourishing, so we wish to understand them accurately. Augustine seems never to misunderstand or misrepresent others' perspectives. At times he seems to understand their social imaginary better than they do. We must put in the effort to hear them. Stephen Covey's famous maxims come to mind: "We look inside our own heads and think we see the world" and "Seek first to understand and then be understood."[14] We must get outside of our own heads, suspend assumptions and judgments, and hear what others are saying.[15]

14. See Covey, "Seek First to Understand," 273–305.

15. For "suspending assumptions," see Senge, *Fifth Discipline*, 243–44.

What can we genuinely affirm?

- The creation story raises challenges in modern times. Christians have differing perspectives on how to read the early chapters of Genesis. No clear consensus has emerged regarding how Genesis 1–3 and recent scientific discoveries coordinate.
- Apparent contradictions exist in Scripture. These conflicts present a challenge to our faith in the veracity of the Bible.
- The church's sexual and financial abuses weaken our confidence that the Spirit of God is truly working in the church.
- Many outside the church live more moral lives than those within it.
- Suffering presents a problem for our faith, and many solutions and explanations do not seem to satisfy. Although many Christians hide it, disappointment with God is a pervasive problem within Christianity.
- We are irrepressibly spiritual beings who hunger for the transcendent. Often we are awestruck by the beauty of creation, and it sometimes takes our breath away. We often sense a presence and long for something more than we can touch, feel, or see.
- Many people who claim to be Christians ignore Jesus's basic teaching in texts like the Sermon on the Mount.
- The world has many good things to enjoy; physical activities are among some of the most delightful.
- People are unique and should live with the grain of who they are and where they are.
- We all have honest questions about the afterlife and what it means for us.
- There are many acts of kindness, works of service, and experiences of friends and family that are deeply meaningful in and of themselves.
- Facing the harsh realities of life is better than avoiding the difficult questions and escaping to a fantasy world of our own imagination.

What Will I Need to Challenge?

We do not need to quickly pivot to challenging what a secular person asserts. While we must challenge certain points of view that late modern skeptics hold, these challenges should happen naturally amid the ebb and flow of a conversation. To sustain interchanges over an extended period and to leave the door open for future interactions, we must not overreact to criticisms of our faith and must avoid trying to correct every error in fact or logic they may put forward. We must patiently, humbly, and lovingly bring up genuine questions related to their thoughts on various matters of life and faith. What authentic questions regarding their perspective arise in your mind as you listen to their point of view?

Most of the questions regarding their perspective will fit under the next diagnostic question, but we must ask ourselves which deeper themes in Gus's assertions we should challenge. For example,

- Can there be true, substantial, and enduring meaning without belief in God?
- Though Christianity does not satisfactorily resolve every instance of suffering, is there another worldview that gives a better answer to the problem of suffering?
- Does science contradict Christianity, or does Christianity provide a theological and philosophical grounding for the practice of science? Doesn't science need a philosophy to support itself, which is itself not science?
- Doesn't Christianity have a long and impressive intellectual tradition? Why do many well-educated intellectuals still believe in the orthodox doctrines of the church and the Bible's authority?
- Is it possible that there is a deeper structure to Scripture that could explain the apparent contradictions?
- Don't logic and reason need a framework in which to function? In this vast universe, where our knowledge is always limited, is there actually an objective view from nowhere? And have our advances in science solved the mysteries of the universe, or have they only opened more mysteries?
- Why does the experience of the natural world sometimes produce within us a sense of awe?
- Isn't what happens to us when we die an urgent and important question worthy of our attention and energy?
- Aren't some experiences of happiness more substantial and enduring than others?
- Is looking within oneself a trustworthy source of morality?
- Wouldn't loving parents make judgments on behalf of their children? Wouldn't a loving God make judgments on what is true and good and what is false and harmful for the world he has made?

Where Does This Story Lead, and Is It Internally Consistent and Livable?

The following questions have the potential to cause Gus to doubt his newfound beliefs and thus create space for reconsidering the Christian story:

- When you left Christianity, did you envision where you were going? Did you just take a leap into the unknown? Sure, there are many unknowns in life, but aren't there many things that we can know? For the biggest questions in life, isn't it important to know some things, like what is good and what is evil, what is meaningful and what is useless, what is harmful and what is productive, what lasts and what fades away?
- Could something—family, service, work, and so on—feel meaningful in the moment but have no larger, substantial meaning in the big scheme of things? And if that is the case, then is it truly meaningful?
- How does life outside of Christianity help people deal with the tragic deaths of their loved ones? Are we as a society falsely comforting ourselves by not asking what happens when we die? Have we made an unspoken pact to be indifferent to these deeper questions and divert our attention to other immediate interests and activities?
- Isn't hypocrisy a human issue, not simply a Christian problem? What worldview could we espouse that does not have people who abuse it or live contrary to its norms?
- Don't casual views toward sex often lead to serious emotional and relational pain? Don't our hearts long for more meaningful encounters with other humans? Should any limits be put on sexual activity? How should we decide on those boundaries?
- How should we decide what success is? How do we know when it is right to limit our ambition? What will help us build more productive and healthy communities rather than just a few successful individuals?
- Where do we find meaning when we lose our ability to experience the great outdoors or work at our dream job?
- What would happen if we all looked within ourselves to determine truth and know what we should do? What would happen if we all expressed our individual desires and lived out our individual dreams? Would societal chaos eventually ensue?
- Does anyone really live in a purely scientific way? Don't we all have faith in something else? Doesn't belief in science involve an act of faith?

At this point, we turn outward. Hopefully, we have listened well and raised questions that created space to share how Christianity is a better story to live in. Perhaps we have caused them to doubt their doubts about Christianity and made them a bit skeptical about their own way of inhabiting the world.

Outside

Where Do the Competing Views Borrow from the Christian Story?

In *Telling a Better Story*, Chatraw makes the important point that Christianity is in the bloodstream of secular society, whether individual skeptics are aware of it or not: "Christianity has been transfused into the bloodstream of Western society. Though your secular friends may oppose Christianity, in many ways it is still pumping through their veins and directly linked to what they see as a healthy society." Chatraw continues with the implications for apologetics: "Your task is to help them see they are likely already personally borrowing from the Christian narrative and to wonder with them what might happen if Christianity—with its assumptions and ethics—were to be completely purged from our culture."[16]

Some of the most dearly held secular beliefs originated with Christianity. So where does Gus borrow from Christianity? Since we cannot always say definitively that points of view developed out of Christianity—this is because God created all people with a sense for the beautiful, good, and true—it may be better to make our points in the form of questions.

- Is it possible that Gus's aversion to sexual and financial abuses results from being brought up in a Western culture formed by the value and respect the Christian Scriptures place on humans?
- Where does the golden rule, with its emphasis on doing good to others and showing kindness to those who are hurting, originate?
- Where would we find a rational and affective framework for finding meaning in doing good to others, contributing at work, and building some significant relationships?
- Does Gus's belief in human freedom have anything to do with Christianity's emphasis on the goodness of free will?
- Has Jesus Christ's rebuke of duplicity and call to honesty shaped Gus's positive attitude toward authenticity?
- Has Christianity's emphasis on the spiritual life inspired Gus's desire to meditate and encounter something out there bigger than himself?

In investigating how one may be borrowing from Christianity, it is possible to link a belief that Gus holds with one that is harder for him to accept.[17] For example, he states that he respects the teaching of Jesus Christ.

16. Chatraw, *Telling a Better Story*, 69. See also Holland, *Dominion*.
17. See Keller, *Center Church*, 119–34.

We might ask, "If you still respect Jesus's teaching, would you consider once again what he says about being a savior? Could you believe Jesus's claim that he died for our sins? Is it possible that his teaching strikes us as unique, authoritative, and good because he is who he claimed to be: the Son of God? Could one who is lying about his identity and mission teach with such insight and power?"

At this point, we have created space to tell a better story. We have entered the story of others and made room for them to consider—or reconsider—Scripture's redemptive narrative. We are ready, as Curtis Chang would say, to retell their story and capture that retold tale within the gospel metanarrative.

How Does the Christian Narrative Better Address Our Experiences, Observations, and History?

This section will be brief, but integrating the redemptive story into our whole story can take a lifetime. The points made here signal larger themes that weave together into a whole-life experience.

Reading through Gus's testimony of deconversion, we could argue that Christianity tells a better story.

A better story about our spiritual journey. His independent Bible church experiences could be considered the opening of the door to his Christian faith. As C. S. Lewis suggests in his book *Mere Christianity*, all Christianity shares a hallway that connects many robust rooms of Christian thought and practice.[18] Christianity has an expansive intellectual and imaginative tradition that includes vast resources of art, music, literature, and thought. A person could spend their life journeying deeper and deeper into the spiritual resources of the Christian story. Gus could conceive his provincial beginning as his first steps into higher plains of spiritual, intellectual, and imaginative exploration. (One has only to follow Augustine on his spiritual, cultural, and theological journey throughout his literary and ministerial growth to see the potential of such expansion and ascension.)

A better story about sex. Gus does not overtly mention sex as a part of his deconversion story, but he seems to imply that his own sexual awakening loosened his commitment to living out the Christian life. The Christian story provides a better structure for sexual flourishing by setting boundaries on sexual activities and by connecting the sex act to the mysteries of female and male differences and human reproduction. Placing sex within a lifetime marital covenant of growing in spiritual, relational, familial, and emotional intimacy takes sex beyond a casual exchange and meaningless pleasure to

18. Lewis, *Mere Christianity*, xv–xvi.

something signifying both the perichoretic nature of the Trinity and the love between Christ and his church.

A better story about vocation. Grounded in the early chapters of Genesis, work is a priestly and kingly vocation of bringing glory to God through tending to God's garden, subduing all things to the reign of God, and ordering creation for the glory of God. Through our vocations, we learn to love God with all our heart, mind, soul, and strength and to love our neighbor as ourselves. Surely thorns and thistles make our work difficult, but knowing that through our work we are advancing God's redemptive reign in this world gives a deeper purpose to our difficult tasks.

A better story about rationality. Rationality is not a given. Logic must have a framework in which to function. The way culture shapes us to imagine the world is certainly *a* rational framework for thinking. But the Christian redemptive story—grounded in the person and work of Jesus Christ and framed in a story of love—provides a universal rationality, a system of logic that can bring in all cultures. As Augustine would assert, everyone looks to some authority to ground their way of being and thinking. The Christian authority framework—primarily exercised through Scripture—provides the rational and revelational structure for reasoning our way through a life of loving God and neighbor.

A better story about science. The Christian story does not contradict science. It grounds it. Christian metaphysics chastens science. It puts science in its proper place, demonstrating that there is more to life than empirical tests can produce. Science matures within a story about a creator who ordered and structured the world to run along expected norms. Creation is not accidental or random but functions purposefully and predictably. Thus, science becomes a study that is not its own end but a way of knowing and loving God, serving others, and fulfilling our vocation on earth.

A better story of human goodness. People are amazingly kind, good, and sacrificial, except when they are not. It is true that humans can be humble and loving, but they can also be hateful, vengeful, self-centered, and cruel. The Christian creation story reveals that humans were created good. They were created in the image of God. As creatures created in God's image, people were made to be self-sacrificial, with a trinitarian love that lives for the other. Jesus expressed the pinnacle of humanity's creational purpose when he laid down his life for others. People were created good, beautiful, and true. But humanity has gone its own way and has turned in on itself, using others for its own benefit and putting itself in the center of its own existence. We have fallen from our original place, yet we have not lost our authentic, creational goodness. Through the redemption of Jesus Christ, believers are being restored to their original goodness, beauty, and truth. We live in accord with who we really are—our authentic selves. Further, God's common grace works in the hearts of those outside the Christian faith to enliven them to some of their creational goodness and to keep them from being as selfish and prideful as they would be otherwise. The Christian story explains more—more of why people can be so good and why they can be so evil.

A better story about the afterlife. The Christian story is a hopeful story with an end like no other. Christianity claims that we have an Edenic memory inside us. We "remember" when we walked with God in the garden. Thus, we long for Eden. We desire the presence of God. We long for peace, a place that is more familiar to our hearts than this foreign and fallen world, a land with no disease, no dying, no wars, no hunger, no loneliness, no disappointment, and no hatred—of ourselves or others. The convincing evidence of the resurrection of Jesus Christ enlivens us with hope beyond this life. This hope energizes our lives toward a meaningful and purposeful life of love for God and others. What we do matters. Our labor is not in vain in the Lord. Commenting on 1 Corinthians 15:58, N. T. Wright assures us, "What you *do* in the present—by painting, preaching, singing, sewing, praying, teaching, building hospitals, digging wells, campaigning for justice, writing poems, caring for the needy, loving your neighbor as yourself—*will last into God's future*."[19] Our lives matter today because who we are and what we do will last forever. The Christian story of hope is a more meaningful, more lasting story.

A better story about freedom. The larger narrative arc of the Bible could be read as a story about freedom. (1) At creation, humankind had a free will. They were free to choose the good and refuse the evil. (2) After the fall, their will was in bondage to sin. Without God's common grace, they could choose only evil. (3) Through the redemption of Jesus Christ, by faith humans regain the possibility of choosing the good and avoiding evil. (4) In the new creation, redeemed humans will be free to choose only the good. This is the ultimate and best type of freedom: the liberated will to choose only the good. This is a story of human flourishing brought about by being freed to freely love. It's a story of being free to do whatever we want and wanting to do what leads to the best life possible: humble love of God and self-sacrificial love of others.[20]

Of course, Augustine used what we would regard today as more typical or traditional apologetics. For example, in *The City of God* he reasons with those skeptical about the possibility of resurrection. He points out that they

19. Wright, *Surprised by Hope*, 193 (italics original).

20. See Han-luen Kantzer Komline's fourfold narrative framework for Augustine's view of the will: (1) the created will, (2) the fallen will, (3) the redeemed will, and (4) the eschatological will. Komline, *Augustine on the Will*.

believe in a God who created the world. Since the world he created is filled with so many wonders, and creation itself is a miracle, why would this creator God not be able to raise the dead?[21] We can see here that Augustine employs an Inside Out approach with an argument from reason.

In another place in *The City of God*, Augustine uses historical evidence for the resurrection combined with a tongue-in-cheek irony. He asserts that people from all over the world—learned and unlearned, noble and common—have come to believe in the resurrection of Jesus Christ and his bodily ascension into heaven. Many came to believe in the resurrection and ascension of Jesus Christ, even though they did not witness the resurrection and ascension with their own eyes, because they were confronted with the many and varied miracles manifested by the apostles. In Augustine's world, the masses have come to believe in these miracles. Yet some are still obstinate and will not believe in these miracles. So satirically Augustine turns the tables with this argument: "But, if they refuse to believe that Christ's apostles really did work these miracles to convince people to believe in their preaching of Christ's resurrection and ascension, they still leave us with this one great miracle—that the whole world has come to believe it without any miracles at all. And that one miracle is enough for us!"[22]

Thus, Augustine used typical apologetic arguments in an ad hoc manner whenever the logic or historical validity of his persuasion was being challenged. Yet the superstructure of his apologetic approach was to go into the conceptual and affectional framework of skeptics, retell a better story of reality, and then capture that retold tale within the gospel metanarrative. Augustine employed a biblically narratival and culturally aware approach. He understood how cultural situatedness shapes how people reason and what they desire. In *Confessions* and *The City of God*, Augustine defends the faith, builds up the confidence of his congregation, and persuades others to the Christian faith. We should do the same for those under our pastoral care. We should teach them how to live out Christ's redemptive story in the place and time in which they find themselves. We should show them how to bear witness to the gospel in a way that connects with their own lives and the lives of the people around them.

Conclusion

It's one thing to articulate a better story for our personal lives and share a gospel witness with those who live among us. But what about living out

21. Augustine, *City of God* 21.7.
22. Augustine, *City of God* 22.5.

our faith in public spaces? With the rise of political divisions and religious pluralism, how do we embody the faith in the public domain? How does the church relate to public spheres like business, education, art, entertainment, and politics? Should we pull back from public life, build up our Christian communities, start our own Christian businesses, build our own educational institutions, do Christian art for ourselves, and avoid the world?

Is our objective for interfacing in public spheres simply to live good lives to build a platform for sharing the gospel? Is evangelism our only substantial reason for interacting with the public? Is the world a sinking ship so that our real objective is to get people in lifeboats? As some have said, "Why polish the brass on a sinking ship?" Why make this world a better place if it is all going to burn up anyway? Let's warn people of what is to come and invite them to place their faith in the gospel.

Or is there more to it than that? Should the church work for the transformation of society? Does living as kingdom citizens involve making a better world, one of peace and justice? Is transforming public spaces participating in the work of God on earth today? Is nurturing the beautiful, good, and true in this world the reason for our vocations?

How does the church relate to public spaces? What part does the pastor play in equipping congregants to live their faith in the public square? Is it possible to live a holistic, integrative public life? Or is it too late? Has our opportunity to live our faith out loud passed in this post-Christian world?

The Christian life is a journey upward. Yet the way of the Christian is not simply personal. Together the church is on an ascending pilgrimage homeward. While on the journey from this world to the next, the pastor equips the people in the church to live out their faith in public spaces. Thus, the final chapter will deal with an Augustinian approach to public theology.

PART FOUR

The Whole Journey

SEVEN

Living in Public Spaces

The Psalms are simultaneously 150 separate spiritual journeys that represent . . . the journeys of our lives, and all 150 psalms connect to various experiences and things that we're going through. But it's also about a single journey. The Psalms are about the journey of Jesus Christ, and he, of course, sings every psalm with us. The incarnation is the greatest example of God's own journey.

—Timothy and Julie Tennent, in "I Have Come to Do Your Will," from *The Wake-Up Call* podcast

When I think what it is that brings us to our Father, it might be grief or sickness—trouble of some sort. Weariness. And then there we are, and it's a good thing at such times to know we have a Father, whose joy it is to welcome us home.

—Marilynne Robinson, *Home*

If Christianity is really true, then it involves the whole man. . . . Christianity is not *just* "dogmatically" true or "doctrinally" true. Rather, it is true to what is there, true in the whole area of the whole man in all of life.

—Francis Schaeffer, *Art and the Bible*

The Journey Homeward

Life is a journey.

Oftentimes Christians think of conversion as that moment when a person repents and believes in Jesus Christ and is born again. But we can understand conversion more broadly by viewing the Christian life as a journey homeward.

When we look at our life as a pilgrimage home to our eternal destiny, conversion can be thought of as a series of changes or a process of transformation that lasts a lifetime. As such, the Christian walk can be experienced as—reimagining the title of Eugene Peterson's enduring book—a long series of conversions in the same direction.[1]

Augustine initially converted to the faith when he heard a voice that sounded like a boy or girl singing repeatedly, "Pick it up and read, pick it up and read." Believing that this was a divine command, he picked up the book of Paul's letters, opened it, and read the first passage he came upon: Romans 13:13–14. The words of the text spoke directly to his heart. He was gloriously converted. Light flooded his heart with assurance of salvation, and peace settled on his face.[2] This is the story of Augustine's initial conversion. We might say that there is one initial conversion to the faith, one original confession of Jesus Christ as Lord, and one once-for-all baptism.

Yet in our journey toward the promised land, we experience many conversions as we live out of our initial conversion and baptism. Salvation is the step-by-step way home as we walk along the path that is Jesus Christ (John 14:6). One destination is in mind, but there are many course corrections. Our spiritual GPS is constantly recalculating. The grace of confession, repentance, and transformation moves us along the path of salvation toward the new heaven and the new earth.

Just when we think we have completed the mental manuscript of our life story—when we perceive that we have understood who we are, who the actors in our story are, and what the events of our lives mean—the divine editor begins to mark through the text of our mental models with red lines, suggesting a different structure, point of view, or way of articulating our experiences. Through his grace, we see where we have been and where we are going with new insight. With humble confidence, we trust the editor and guide of our lives. Conversion is a process begun at some point in time, but it continues repeatedly in new and fresh ways throughout our journey. It was a process of conversions for Augustine; it will be so for us and the people we shepherd. We progress in trusting our guide with increasing confidence, knowing ourselves more deeply, and walking more discerningly.

The Process of Conversion and *Augustine's* Expositions of the Psalms

When we encounter Augustine's digressions in his sermons for the first time, we may conclude that he is not making any progress but is wandering

1. Peterson, *Long Obedience in the Same Direction*.
2. Augustine, *Confessions* 8.11.29–30.

around in the wilderness, going nowhere. Michael Cameron thinks otherwise. In his introduction to *Essential Expositions of the Psalms by Saint Augustine*, Cameron explains the coherence and purposefulness of Augustine's apparent ramblings in his exegesis and preaching:

> I suggest that if we patiently watch Augustine work at his craft of exegesis and preaching, a subtle pattern begins to suggest itself, *a pattern formed by the process of conversion*. It begins to appear that he constructed the episodes of exegesis to stir in hearers and readers a continual movement of spiritual change, and that the format of running exegesis had something to do with that. He pursued a process that led people to undertake a journey even more than merely to learn a map. He worked to stir up the restless heart of his congregation to seek rest in God by bringing them out of the grandstands and into the arena of wrestling with Scripture. This exegetical process kept hearers' hearts seeking and their spiritual feet moving in transit to God, not outwardly but inwardly, as Augustine never tired of repeating (e.g., 119,1). Thus each episode of exegesis was training. It was a set of exercises that coached hearts up the steps of ascent toward spiritual love and commitment.[3]

Augustine viewed Christ himself—the path—as the organizing center of the entire Bible. Reading and rereading the Scriptures recalibrates our life and reshapes our inner world, a lifelong process of soul shaping. Augustine never saw himself as more than just beginning in his understanding of Scripture and in his journey down the path. In a letter, he admits to a friend that he is always just beginning:

> For the depth of the Christian writings is so great that I would daily make progress in them if I tried with the greatest leisure, the highest desire, and greater talent to master them alone from the beginning of boyhood up to decrepit old age. It is not that one comes to those matters that are necessary for salvation with such great difficulty, but, though each person grasps in them the faith without which one does not live a pious and upright life, there remain to be understood by those making progress so many things, and things cloaked with so many shadows of mysteries, and there lies hidden so great a depth of wisdom, not only in the words by which they are stated in that way but also in the realities that are to be understood, that those who are the oldest, the most intelligent, and the most ardent with the desire to learn, experience what the same scripture says in another passage, *When a human being has come to the end, he is then at the beginning* (Sir 18:6).[4]

3. Cameron, introduction, 16–17 (italics original).
4. Augustine, *Letters* 137.1.3 (italics original).

Commenting on this text, Cameron writes,

> [Augustine is] concerned to develop a *skill in reading Scripture* that is closely tied to his sense of its purpose in bringing about conversion. "Conversion" here refers not to a moment but to a process of change; it means not only initially entering upon the life of faith but also continually "making progress" in attaining spiritual wisdom. It follows that Augustine's conversion-oriented exegesis would constantly return to the same themes of salvation and community, even as he continually turns the knobs on Scripture's kaleidoscope of images that relate to Christ and the Church, orienting everything toward the embrace of divine love that is conversion.[5]

We walk along the path of Christ by reading and rereading Scripture in the church. As the Holy Spirit illuminates the text of Scripture for us, we advance along the path homeward through the process of conversion. We read and reread Scripture, and Scripture reads and rereads us. Through these many conversions, reading the Scriptures with the church opens our minds and hearts to fresh readings of our own personal journey.

The Psalms of Ascent

The Psalms of Ascent or "the Step-Song collection (Pss 119–133) was a sort of doorway into the great house of the Psalter," Cameron asserts. He continues, "Its stairway imagery fit well with the trajectory of spiritual ascent at the center of Augustine's conversion-oriented thought and spirituality. . . . Though its upward journey will end only in the future life, the soul makes a genuine beginning here below, fueled by liturgy, sacraments, humility, grace, prayer, the practice of love—and reading Scripture in community."[6] The whole Christ reads the whole Scriptures together for the whole journey upward.

Our ascent is a journey of the heart. At the very beginning of the Psalms of Ascent, Augustine gives a general introduction. He explains, "Now ascents, steps, can be used for either going up or going down, but the steps that appear in these psalms represent people going up. We too are to ascend, but we must not try to climb with our bodily feet; rather should we remember what was written in another psalm: *God arranges ascents in his heart, in the valley of weeping, to the place he has appointed* (Ps 83:6–7 (84:5–6)). *Ascents*, it is said. Where? In the heart. What is the starting point? The valley of weeping.

5. Cameron, introduction, 18 (italics original).

6. Cameron, introduction, 44–45. In the Masoretic Text of the Hebrew Bible, these are Pss. 120–34, which were sung by Jewish pilgrims on their way to worship in Jerusalem.

But wither are we mounting?"[7] The answer is hard to say or, better, impossible to say. Augustine imagines the Holy Spirit speaking to us: "Can anyone comprehend where we shall be after the present life, if we have ascended in our hearts? No, no one; and you will do better to hope for a place of happiness beyond all telling, which he who arranged ascents in your heart has appointed for you."[8] What Augustine does know is that the starting point of our ascent, the mountain that we must climb, the sustenance for our trek, the path that we must take with one another, and the goal that we ascend to are all our Lord Jesus Christ.[9] The ascent begins with humble weeping and ends with eternal happiness beyond words. Along the way, we are transformed by Christ's healing and wisdom. We are converted and being converted. Again, he is our doctor and our teacher.

We are on a pilgrimage with the church as it travels ever upward toward its eternal dwelling. At this destination, the church will experience total health. In contrast, healing does not happen instantaneously in this phase of our existence. Those who are brought to the inn of God's healing are never completely restored in this life. Although the path toward healing in Jesus Christ ascends toward full recovery, the church never leaves its suffering and sickness completely behind. The church is perpetually reorienting—or converting, if you will—toward loving God and loving one another. We are a church in recovery, taking our daily doses of medication with our eyes cast upward toward the great physician and complete healing in our eternal home. In our journey, the church is like a hospital.

In our pilgrimage homeward, the church is also like a school. In this ecclesial school, we learn wisdom. It's a school we never graduate from—not until we arrive home—but we do ascend the steps of this school one grade at a time. Through spiritual conversions, we advance in true wisdom. Wisdom in this school is spiritual understanding advanced through knowledge and transfigured by love of the eternal.[10] God does not advance or change. Augustine explains, "Wisdom resides in knowing and loving him who abides eternally beyond all change, God."[11] Yet we change and progress in our knowledge and love of him.

As noted, in this church-school—the whole Christ—individuals are at different stages in their development. In their educational ascent, they stand on different steps. The preacher and the congregation as Christ's body help each

7. Augustine, *Expositions of the Psalms* 119.1 (italics original).
8. Augustine, *Expositions of the Psalms* 119.1.
9. Augustine, *Expositions of the Psalms* 119.1, 2.
10. Cameron, introduction, 40.
11. Augustine, *Expositions of the Psalms* 135.8.

person to take the next step in the ascent homeward. Cameron likens the congregation to "a one-room schoolhouse wherein a single instructor teaches at several levels simultaneously, while students imitate and instruct one another."[12]

Frameworks for Pastoring Pilgrims on Their Upward Journey

In his exposition of the first psalm of ascent, Augustine provides two interrelated frameworks for pastoring the congregation in their journey up the steps toward home. The first involves his interpretation and application of Jacob's ladder. In Jacob's vision of the ladder, some were ascending and some were descending the ladder. In Jesus Christ, God descended the ladder in human flesh, thus accommodating the Word to our frail humanity. To heal and teach us, Christ came down. In descending, God makes himself articulate so that little ones can come to know the Great One. Augustine explains why we need Christ's descent:

> "We speak in a fashion you can understand." And this was because Christ also, by being born and suffering, made himself such that people could talk about him; for humans easily talk about another human. Can any mortal talk about God, as God truly is? But men and women readily speak about someone human like themselves. If great people were to come down to little ones and yet speak to them only of him who is great, it was necessary for him who was great to become little himself, so that great human teachers could speak of him to little people. And this he did.[13]

Following Christ in his descent, teachers and preachers must come down, accommodating their teaching to where people are. We ask ourselves, "How can I connect my teaching with the step they are standing on in their ascent home? Where are they on their journey? What insight from Scripture will it take to move them forward?"

At this point, we must introduce Augustine's second framework for pastoring a congregation at different stages in their ascent homeward. This framework involves understanding different groups and where they stand on the various rungs of the ladder. Augustine identifies three groups in his exposition of the first psalm of ascent: *little ones*, *climbers*, and *spirituals*.

- Who are the little ones? These are those who need solid food but must first take in milk. As the Word, Jesus Christ is solid food, but he feeds

12. Cameron, introduction, 43.
13. Augustine, *Expositions of the Psalms* 119.2.

spiritual infants with the milk of his flesh, like a mother digests solid food and feeds it to her little one. So too must teachers digest the solid food and feed it to infants. And the little ones must receive the milk with humility in "the valley of weeping."

- Who are the climbers? They are those who are making progress up the rungs of the ladder toward a better understanding of spiritual things.
- Who are the spirituals? Those who descend the ladder accommodating their teaching to those at lower levels, particularly the little ones.[14]

This framework helps the pastor and teacher understand that the members of a congregation are not all on the same level of ascent. This enables church leaders to avoid lumping everyone together into one mass. Contrary to a flat view of the congregation, people are at different stages. They stand on different steps in the ascending journey home, so pastors and teachers must accommodate their ministry and teaching to the different groups. For some in the congregation, the teacher must descend the stairway—or ladder—to shepherd and speak to those at lower levels. Cameron emphasizes how these groups help us see, catalyze, measure, and accommodate the needs of each group: "These categories are lenses through which to see, and against which to measure, the restless movement of conversion Augustine hoped to catalyze. . . . Augustine structured the steps of spiritual conversion . . . , explicitly addressing the needs of particular hearers. Thus the *Expositions* maintained awareness of the larger constellation of Christian convictions and values while negotiating the rhetorical situation with specific groups by accommodation and decorum."[15]

Perhaps you have preached or taught in a sanctuary or classroom with stadium seating. Imagine such a room with the little ones seated in the first couple rows at the bottom. The climbers make up the largest section in the middle. Further, the climbers are seated at various levels according to the progress they have made on their ascent homeward. The spirituals are seated at the top. In preaching or teaching to a congregation like this, we must accommodate our message or lesson to the various levels. Our aim is to catalyze each person's next step upward in their conversion process.

A couple words of caution: First, it's important not to harden the categories. These groups are permeable and flexible. Unless we become like little ones, we will in no way enter the kingdom of God. This disposition is required of all Christians, no matter the level. Even if we make great progress

14. Augustine, *Expositions of the Psalms* 119.2.

15. Cameron, introduction, 43–44.

in the process of conversion, we are always just beginning as we reimagine and reconceive the faith and our place in it. Using the one-room schoolhouse analogy, the learned spirituals must come down to teach the little ones and the climbers. The climbers also have lessons to teach the little ones because they are closer to where the little ones are. Yet each level has something to offer the others. Little ones will oftentimes teach the spirituals and climbers new lessons. And as we all know, we learn best by teaching others.

Second, the pastor must be careful not to put faces in these categories, since this is God's work of grace. Too often those who are regarded as "mature" believers because they have more knowledge and experience in the church are experts at hiding dark secrets in their private worlds and twisted motives in their hearts. Sure, we know when a person is new to the faith or only recently baptized. They are obviously little ones, but they must be treated with honor and respect. Truly they bring new perspectives and fresh insights that may add value to the upward ascent of even the spirituals.

Taking Steps Together

Last Sunday afternoon—as of the time I write this chapter—my wife and I stood in the emergency room beside the bed of George. George is eighty-two. For four months he has alternated between the hospital and rehab facilities. Although a stroke slurred his speech for a while and bleeding diverticulitis has weakened his body, George's mind and memory are still sharp on most days. Recently he recounted his life story to my wife. His story reads like the headings of a book: "Orphaned and on My Own," "Adopted by a Preacher," "Military School," "Escape on a Train and the Loss of a Friend," "This Life Isn't So Bad," "The Reluctant Lawyer," "Partnership and Nonprofits," "Reprise with Carolyn."

In the emergency room, George, who has fought valiantly with a positive attitude to live, shared with us that he doesn't think he has much longer. When he began to speak of his demise, I drew close to him and looked deeply into his eyes. I wanted to see into the soul of this dying man and hear the depth of his words. He spoke of his exhaustion. He's tired of the struggle to live. He's not afraid to die and seems ready to go. And he's hopeful that Carolyn, his wife, will be OK. Surprisingly, he spoke of snow cones, chocolate milk—he was parched—and the Golden Corral. Mid-conversation, he dozed off and began to sleep comfortably. I visited him again on Thursday. He was asleep then too. I gently called his name several times, but he continued to sleep, so I let him rest. I prayed over him and left. George is a beautiful soul. He calls Karen and me friends, assures us of his love for us every time we visit him, and tells others how much he appreciates us. George is on his way home, but in truth, he has been on a journey homeward throughout his life. He has been making that ascent step-by-step. His story is unique, like no other. Yet he is on a path that is common to all of us.

I pastor an older church in a small town. It's a smallish church, but I do many funerals for a church of that size. I appreciate the opportunity that God has given me to honor so many church members by performing their funerals. Sometimes I think that is the primary reason God has called me to this place. I am happy that he would trust me that way.

But there are many young families in the church as well. In the next couple of months, we will hire a youth minister, a newly created position. Our church is growing younger.

The point is every person in our church—young, middle-aged, and elderly—is going the way of George. They are at different places, but they are all on the same path. Our ministry to them is to help them be intentional and have a telos, a goal that focuses them homeward. Sometimes we will have the insight to discern where a certain pilgrim is on their journey, but oftentimes we are better off leaving that judgment to the discerner of their hearts. Yet we can design our church ministries, our preaching, and our pastoral care to help others take the next step in their ascent toward a deeper love of God and realization of who he is.

Early in my ministry, I was uncomfortable in my own skin. I felt awkward speaking in front of people (a large deficit for a pastor) and uptight in many social settings. I was noticeably anxious and insecure, though I was desperate to manage it so that others wouldn't see it—but it was obvious to spiritually mature and emotionally stable people. My mind moved frantically from one nervous thought to the next and from one ministry idea to another. Although most folks thought I was "nice," I had a very strong will and needed to be in control of my world.

During this time, a fellow in our church named Steve gave me a book by David Runcorn titled *A Center of Quiet*. I no longer have the book and remember almost nothing specific about its content, except that it introduced me to a world of spiritual disciplines that, in my Baptist background, I had not seriously considered before—disciplines like centering my mind on Jesus Christ through solitude and silence. I began to practice sitting in silence, at first for short periods of time, like five minutes, and then for longer stretches, like days. I became more aware of God's work in my inner world. Negative emotions became like warning lights on the dashboard of my inner engine, letting me know when I was running on the wrong passions, especially anger, fear, and anxiety. Jesus Christ began a fresh work of healing the sinful—primarily my own sin but also the sin of others against me—woundedness of my soul. This opened a new world to me of contemplative prayer and other spiritual practices. Steve cared for me, and he helped me take an important step forward in my ascent homeward. I was converted to a new level in my spiritual life.

Phil also helped me take a step upward in my spiritual leadership. Feeling discouraged after a church leadership meeting, I leaned against my car in the darkness and declared to Phil, "I'm not a leader." Phil responded, "Yes, you are. You're just a different kind of leader." Phil was unusually wise for a guy in his mid-twenties. Today, I don't remember much about the rest of the conversation, but I do recall that the next morning when I got up early to go into the office, I discovered a book on my front porch. Phil had gone to Books-A-Million after our conversation and had bought and placed it there. I took the book into my office and read every word of it that day. It's the best book I have ever read on leadership. Thirty-five years after I found the book on my front porch, I still have it, and I still go back and reread the sections that I underlined that day. The name of the book? *In the Name of Jesus: Reflections on Christian Leadership* by Henri Nouwen. Phil helped me take a step forward in my spiritual leadership. I was converted to a new, fresh way of leading in the name of Jesus. Phil discerned the next step I needed to take.

Like in a one-room schoolhouse, we have others in church who help us take the next step in our ascent. As pastors, we have not arrived. To help others on the journey, we must be hopeful climbers ourselves.

As pastors, we can't just say, "Take two books and call me in the morning," like the key to the next step in the journey is always another book. Books are my love language. But they are not everyone's love language. As ministers we can ask God to guide us and our churches into discerning how to help others move onward and upward on the path toward healing and wisdom. How can we support them as they take their next step in the journey? What can we do to motivate them to persevere on the journey when they are not sure where to go or how to get there? One size does not fit all, but through the grace and leadership of God, we can create a culture of ascent homeward.

A Hopeful Journey in Public Spaces

Ministers should shepherd their congregation along a hopeful journey home.

One danger of the ascent is the obsession with arriving. Some of us intensely long for completeness and closure. We want to put a bow on our journey and live happily ever after, perhaps with lasting moral perfectionism, an enduring spiritual high, an airtight theological system, or an unassailable ecclesial tradition. Some of us have a longing for everything to be settled. We want to rest, relax, and exhale, saying, "We have arrived. We are home."

But we are not home yet. As Augustine would say regarding Psalm 119, we are still in exile. He imagines the psalmist saying:

> "*Alas, alas, how long-drawn-out is my exile!* I have gone so far away from you. My pilgrimage is so wearisome! I have not yet arrived in that homeland where I shall live untroubled by any evil. Not yet have I attained to the fellowship of the angels, where I shall have no scandals to dread. Why am I not yet there? Because *my exile is so long-drawn-out*." An exile implies a pilgrimage or journey abroad. A person who lives in a foreign land, away from his own country, is called an exile. Thus the psalmist laments, *How long-drawn-out is my exile!* And where is he, in this prolonged exile?[16]

This is the cry of an individual, but it is more accurately the lament of the whole Christ throughout the world. Augustine explains,

> But what of the psalmist; what has he to say? *How long-drawn-out is my exile!* This is definitely the voice of pilgrims and exiles, the voice of the Church as it struggles along on earth. It is the voice of one who cries out from far-off countries in another psalm: *From the ends of the earth I have called to you* (Ps 60:3(61:2)). Is there any one of us who cries from the ends of the earth? No: not I, nor you, nor he, nor she; but the whole Church cries from the ends of the earth.[17]

We cry out because we are still homesick, because we have not arrived at the shore of our eternal happiness. Still, we are hopeful and happy now; we are happy in hope. The church throughout the world is on a pilgrimage toward eternal happiness. In its exilic state, the church is happy in that hope. Augustine explains this in *The City of God*:

> If anyone uses this life in such a way that he directs it to that other life as the end which he loves with ardent intensity and for which he hopes with unwavering faithfulness, it is not absurd to call him happy even now, although *happy in that hope* rather than in this reality. Without that hope, in fact, this reality is only a false happiness and a great misery. For it does not make use of the true goods of the soul, because no wisdom is true wisdom if it does not direct its intention—in everything that it discerns with prudence, bears with fortitude, constrains with temperance, and distributes with justice—to the end where God will be all in all in assured eternity and perfect peace.[18]

16. Augustine, *Expositions of the Psalms* 119.6 (italics original).
17. Augustine, *Expositions of the Psalms* 119.7 (italics original).
18. Augustine, *City of God* 19.20 (italics added).

We are a hopeful church, exiled in this world but hopeful of the world to come. The journey is not simply one of the heart. We are on an embodied journey in a real world that is moving toward redemption and re-creation, a new heaven and earth. Faith is not simply private but public. Augustine pastored a church on pilgrimage in a certain time and a specific place. Oftentimes he was burdened with civic administrative duties. In his everyday practice, his faith was public. He preferred a monastery in the city.

Augustine's journey included the church's hopeful and happy journey in public spaces. Though Augustine always kept the distinction clear between the city of God and the city of man, he envisioned and practiced an active participation in the public square. He envisioned the hopeful journey of the church bringing shared happiness into civic life, not by dominating or "winning" but by living out the faithful journey in shared spaces. Augustine raises our diminished contemporary expectations for the possibilities of a Christian ruler's influence for the common good:

> We call Christian emperors happy if they rule justly; if they do not swell with pride among the voices of those who honor them too highly and the obsequiousness of those who acclaim them too humbly, but remember that they are only human beings; if they make their power the servant of God's majesty, using it to spread the worship of God as much as possible; if they fear, love, and worship God; if, more than their own kingdom, they love the one where they do not fear to have co-rulers; if they are slow to punish and quick to pardon; . . . if they do all this not out of a craving for empty glory but rather out of love for eternal happiness; and if, for their sins, they do not neglect to offer their true God the sacrifice of humility and compassion and prayer. It is Christian emperors such as this that we say are happy. For the present, they are happy in hope; hereafter, they will be happy in reality, when that to which we now look forward has actually arrived.[19]

Augustine does not advise a retreat from influencing the public square in the here and now, nor does he recommend a quietism that keeps one's faith merely private. Rather, he recognizes that the happy emperor—one who is happy and brings this happy hope into the public square—is the one who lives faith out loud with a humble boldness. Augustine's words do not apply merely to emperors but to presidents, governors, legislators, mechanics, entrepreneurs, educators, engineers, artists, financial planners, musicians, doctors, plumbers, and the whole gamut of vocations in public spaces.

19. Augustine, *City of God* 5.24.

Living in public spaces—especially within our pluralistic society today—produces such difficulties that it is often tempting to retreat into the safety of our ecclesial tribe. But using the insightful phrase "live ahead of time," Augustine counsels us not to withdraw into an insular tribe. In a letter to Boniface, a Christian general who later became the count of Africa, Augustine advises, "But because in this world it is necessary that the citizens of the kingdom of heaven suffer temptations among those who are in error and are wicked so that they may be exercised and put to the test like gold in a furnace, we ought not to want to live ahead of time with only the saints and the righteous."[20] Living our faith out loud in public spaces has a sanctifying effect on us and, hopefully, on those common places, especially when we demonstrate faith, hope, and love in the "mixed-up" or pluralistic realm. In a sermon warning his congregation about the dangers of a public faith, Augustine exhorts his congregation toward living their faith out loud anyway:

> So if you believe, hope, and love, it doesn't mean that you are immediately to be declared safe and sound and saved. It makes a difference, you see, what you believe, what you hope for, what you love. Nobody in fact can live any style of life without those three sentiments of the soul, of believing, hoping, loving. If you don't believe what the nations believe, and don't hope for what the nations hope for, and don't love what the nations love, then you are gathered from among the nations. And don't let your being physically mixed up with them alarm you, when there is such a wide separation of minds. What after all could be so widely separated as that they believe demons are gods, you on the other hand believe in the God who is the true God? That they hope for the vanities of this age, you hope for eternal life? That they love the world, you love the world's architect.
>
> So if you believe something different from them, hope for something different, love something different, you should prove it by your life, demonstrate it by your actions.[21]

How do we as pastors help the congregation live out its faith in the public square? How do we support the congregation in its public life? How do we avoid creating a kind of dualism, with two different realms—Christian and secular—that have very little to do with each other, two realms that we must switch back and forth between? Or how do we show them a different way than withdrawing from influencing a pluralistic society?

Here are three suggestions to help those in our churches live out their happy-in-hope journey in the public square.

20. Augustine, *Letters* 189.5.

21. Augustine, *Sermons* 198.2.

Cultural Exegesis as Pastoral Ministry

First, be a cultural exegete.

Pastors must learn how to discern and unmask the false narratives and cultural practices that are shaping their congregants. How is the culture—especially the local culture—shaping the beliefs, the hopes, and the loves of the people of our community? James K. A. Smith suggests that the pastor should "serve a congregation by being an ethnographer of the rites of the empire that surround it." He advises pastors to teach the congregation to "read the rituals" of their late modern context. This is not easy to do. It takes intentionality. Smith emphasizes that "it requires thoughtful, rigorous, theological work to pierce through the everyday rituals we go through on autopilot and see them for what they are: ways we are lulled into paying homage to rival kings." Further, this work "is an essentially *local*, contextualized task, both in time and in space: the political idolatries that tempt us and threaten to deform us are localized."[22]

My wife, Karen, and I grew up as Baptists, and until recently I had pastored only nondenominational Baptistic churches. I also work in a university that grew out of a Baptist church. So when we visited a small Anglican church in our community, it was an entirely different experience. Granted, I had attended Roman Catholic services when I was studying at Notre Dame, but this was different. It was an evangelical catholic church, and we were warmly welcomed to take the sacraments. Although this little church was biblical and evangelical at heart, it was still heavy on liturgy and tradition with no "relevant" contemporary songs or loud musical performances.

After the service, as Karen and I walked out to our car, she turned to me and said, "Well, that wasn't about us." No, it wasn't about us. It was a performance all right, but one done for God, not for us.

But God did something in the service. After attending a few times, I realized something was being done to us. We were being re-storied. Through the liturgies, God was forming us into a different narrative. These biblical and traditional (tested over time) liturgies exposed the false cultural narratives and liturgies that have daily shaped our beliefs, hopes, and loves—narratives of upward mobility; self-fulfillment; academic accomplishment; impressive titles; financial freedom; social capital; cultural sophistication; business, academic, sports, political, and entertainment hero worship; and national dominance. These are the things that we (I) so often believe in, hope for, and love. We also have liturgies that shape us for participation in cultural narratives—liturgies like Super Bowls, awards ceremonies, patriotic holidays, end-of-year raises

22. J. K. A. Smith, *Awaiting the King*, 194–95 (italics original).

and bonuses, coveted promotions, online shopping, bingeing Netflix, owning luxury SUVs, wearing the latest clothing styles, working out at elite gyms, watching home renovation shows, taking envied vacations, and so on. We need to advance and acquire things that are bigger, better, and newer.

These cultural narratives and liturgies are made apparent when contrasted to the trinitarian-shaped story advanced in the Apostles' Creed, the "our Father" and "hallowed be thy name" of the Lord's Prayer, the confession of sin and of the unworthiness of our souls, the centeredness of the gospel in the service, the preaching and reading of authoritative Scriptures, the blending of our voices in reading together the Psalms, the theologically rich but musically humble singing to God, and finally, the kneeling with hands cupped like a beggar, waiting to be fed with the mysteries of the body and blood of Jesus. As my son told me, "You can truly sense the temperature of the waters you are in only by moving to other waters."

This is cultural exegesis. The pastor needs to resist cultural captivity; that is, the shepherds of God's flock need to be personally aware of the way cultural narratives and liturgies shape their beliefs, hopes, and loves. Then, they can use the liturgies, along with their teaching and preaching, to unmask the cultural narratives that the members of the congregation live in every day and to re-story and re-form—convert, if you will—the congregation to higher levels of living in their personal lives and public spaces. The pastor, as a cultural exegete, helps redirect and reorder the loves of congregants toward God and neighbor.

Virtue Formation for Engagement in the Public Square

Second, consciously help the congregants form the virtue necessary to live out their faith in public spaces.

Equip the saints to be better church members *and* better citizens. Through God's grace, the liturgies and sacraments have the power to shape Christians into more virtuous soccer coaches, patriots, school board members, teachers, plumbers, and mayors. Through preaching and teaching, along with fully engaging in these holy practices and mysteries personally, the pastor leads in forming private and public virtues within the congregation. The public virtue-forming telos is the coming of the kingdom of God. The journey is the ascent toward total realization of the will of God, which—as Augustine would be ever careful to remind us—will not be reached until Jesus returns. And though we have chastened expectations, we still grow in the virtues of the kingdom for the here and now and for the public spaces we inhabit.

For example, praying the Lord's Prayer in public spaces—as well as encouraging private recitations of the Lord's Prayer—is key to developing a healthy public vision and forming the personal virtue necessary to engage in public spaces Christianly. Oliver O'Donovan recognizes the prayer's "importance as a training in the active life, an ordering of practical thought."[23] Praying the prayer indicates that the church wants to become the kind of kingdom people who live out the life of the kingdom in public spaces. N. T. Wright explains, "We can only pray this prayer for the church if we are prepared to mean: make us Kingdom-bearers! Make us a community of healed healers; make us a retuned orchestra to play the Kingdom music until the world takes up the song. Make us, in turn, Servants of the Lord, the few with the message for the many."[24]

Referring to the recitation of the Lord's Prayer in "religious services and daily rituals," along with how the prayer in its ecclesial repetitions is "both a spiritual and social practice," Michael Lamb explains how the Lord's Prayer habituates Christians toward properly ordered hope: "With enough time and repetition, such a practice can help participants develop a virtue or habit that reflects properly ordered hope. As a result, the Lord's Prayer is . . . a moral, spiritual, and social practice whose repetition can enable practitioners to reorder their hopes."[25]

Augustine recognizes the connection between the eternal and the temporal in the Lord's Prayer: "What we ask for when we say, *Hallowed be your name, your kingdom come, your will be done, on earth as it is in heaven* (Mt 6:9–10) . . . are certainly gifts that we must keep permanently: they begin here and as we progress they grow in us, but once they are perfect, which is something we must hope for in the next life, they will be possessed forever."[26]

The Lord's Prayer helps us form eternal virtues—the virtues of Christ, since he also prayed and practiced this prayer—for temporal life in the public square. Again, Lamb emphasizes both the virtue and the importance of temporal goods: "Augustine encourages audiences not only to learn a practice but also to imitate an exemplar, to model one who exemplifies properly ordered faith, hope, and love. . . . In encouraging Christians to imitate Christ's prayer, Augustine is teaching them not only *what* to hope for, but *how* to hope, namely, in the way that Christ hoped. . . . Even Christ was not so focused on eternal goods that he ignored the need to hope for temporal goods during his earthly life. Christ's example fits with an Augustinian order of hope that allows hope for temporal goods."[27]

23. O'Donovan, *Self, World, and Time*, 39–40.
24. Wright, *Lord and His Prayer*, 32.
25. Lamb, *Commonwealth of Hope*, 60.
26. Augustine, *Enchiridion on Faith, Hope, and Charity* 30.115 (italics original).
27. Lamb, *Commonwealth of Hope*, 62 (italics original).

As the church makes its ascent to the eternal realities it hopes for, it begins to experience these realities now, in private and public. Praying and living the Lord's Prayer shapes our virtue for engagement in public spaces.

Proximate Goods in Shared Spaces

Third, inspire the members of the congregation to work for the common good, peace, and human flourishing in public spaces.

One of the many reasons I welcomed the opportunity to pastor the church I am now serving is their purpose statement: "to make disciples of Jesus Christ for the transformation of the world." In our local context, I imagine this to mean (1) increasing the levels of human flourishing, (2) expanding shared good, and (3) growing the number of disciples of Jesus Christ. We engage in the public square not just to show everyone how they are wrong but to show how they can be made right.[28] We are on a healing project, converting communities to the upward way. In *To Change the World*, James Davison Hunter uses the term "faithful presence" to connect Christian virtue with the transformation of the world: "In short, faithful presence in practice is the exercise of leadership in all spheres and all levels of life and activity. It represents a quality of commitment oriented to the fruitfulness, wholeness, and well-being of all."[29]

We must have a realistic view of how much good we can bring about in public spaces. In this saeculum—the time between now and the new heaven and the new earth—Augustine would warn us against an overreaching or over-realized eschatology. The heavenly city has not come in its eternal fullness, but in the way Augustine lived, in the treatises he dictated, in the sermons he preached, in the prayers he prayed, and in the letters he wrote as a bishop, we see that he advocated for the common good in civic life. The eternal hope of the heavenly city inspires temporal hope for the life of the earthly city. Kristen Deede Johnson asserts that "the earthly city can, then, achieve limited goods, even if not the greatest goods for which humankind was created. And citizens of the Heavenly City can help foster those goods in the many different earthly cities in which they find themselves." Simply put, "even the most disordered persons and institutions do not fall outside of the providence of God."[30]

The welfare of public spaces is good for all, those of the earthly city and those of the heavenly city. We work for the common good of the city, just

28. I am in debt to Charles Mathewes for emphasizing this point in his lectures. Mathewes, *Books That Matter.*

29. Hunter, *To Change the World*, 260.

30. Johnson, *Theology, Political Theory, and Pluralism*, 169.

as the Israelites were instructed to seek the welfare of Babylon (Jer. 29:7).[31] Commenting on Jeremiah's call for the Israelites to work for the good of the city, James Davison Hunter writes, "He was calling them to maintain their distinctiveness as a community but in ways that served the common good."[32] James K. A. Smith adds, "We shouldn't shrink from hoping to bend our policy and public rituals in the direction of rightly ordered love, not so we can 'win' or 'be in control,' but for the sake of our neighbors, for the flourishing of the poor and vulnerable, for the common good."[33] O'Donovan suggests that the common goods that the rule of God in Christ brings to bear on society leave lasting marks in our public life together: "Like the surface of a planet pocked with craters by the bombardment it receives from space, the governments of the passing age show the impact of Christ's dawning glory."[34] This happens at the national and international level but occurs locally as well. What kingdom craters are our churches creating in their local communities? What public policies are we bending in the direction of rightly ordered love? Is our church making a positive difference in our local context? Are our mission efforts transforming public spaces? Are we doing our neighbors any good?

Lamb identifies these goods not as ultimate—in the sense of the goods of the city of God in eternity—but as "proximate." Referring to these goods as "common objects of love," Lamb writes, "Importantly, Augustine does not cast these 'common objects' simply as ultimate or otherworldly ends. Rather, these common objects include proximate, this-worldly goods, the 'good things appropriate to this life.'"[35]

For Augustine, the highest proximate good is peace:

> God is, therefore, the supremely wise creator and the supremely just orderer of all natures. He established the mortal human race as earth's highest ornament, and he bestowed on human beings certain goods suited to this life, namely, a temporal peace appropriate to the brief measure of a mortal life, consisting in bodily health and soundness, and the society of one's own kind, as well as whatever is necessary to maintain or recover this peace (such as those things which are readily and conveniently on hand for our senses—light, speech, air to breathe, water to drink—and whatever is suited to feeding, clothing, healing, and adorning the body).[36]

31. J. K. A. Smith, *Awaiting the King*, 219.
32. Hunter, *To Change the World*, 278.
33. J. K. A. Smith, *Awaiting the King*, 34.
34. O'Donovan, *Desire of the Nations*, 212.
35. Lamb, *Commonwealth of Hope*, 181, quoting Augustine, *City of God* 19.13.
36. Augustine, *City of God* 19.13.

These are proximate goods, common objects of love. We legitimately hope for all people to share in these goods, especially peace. Jean Bethke Elshtain claims in *Augustine and the Limits of Politics*, "An imperfect but nonetheless real earthly peace lies within the realm of the possible." Elshtain's relative peace sounds similar to Lamb's concept of proximate goods when Elshtain writes, "But our life of fellowship . . . calls us, not to perfection, but to relative peace. The Heavenly City is a perfect vision of peace. But there is earthly work to be done in the name of peace."[37]

Yet Augustine masterfully and hopefully connects our sharing of proximate goods and our work for relative peace to ultimate goods and eternal peace. God provided the conditions for a relative peace for an ultimate reason: "He did this, however, on the wholly just condition that any mortal who makes right use of such goods, which are meant to serve the peace of mortals, will receive fuller and better goods, namely, the peace of immortality and the glory and honor appropriate to it, in an eternal life meant for the enjoyment of God and of one's neighbor in God, but that anyone who uses them wrongly will not receive these eternal goods and in fact will lose those temporal goods."[38]

Over the past year, our church has engaged in virtue-forming and world-transforming activities:

- We observed the seasons of the church calendar and virtue-forming liturgies to shape us into hopeful transformers of our local world who bring proximate goods into the workplace and spheres of influence.
- We prayed the Lord's Prayer together at least once a week.
- We held our annual Feeding Appomattox Day on Thanksgiving. This past year we fed over three hundred people in our community.
- We gave away seven hundred bottles of water at our town's annual railroad festival.
- We sent eighty-four shoeboxes to Operation Christmas Child.
- We held Community Give Back Day in our gym.
- We are starting a drive-by food pantry in our church parking lot.
- We assisted forty-six people in our community with emergencies, providing things such as utility bills, short-term housing, and groceries.
- We sponsored a community revival in our sanctuary that brought together over twenty different churches in various denominations.

37. Elshtain, *Augustine and the Limits of Politics*, 105.
38. Augustine, *City of God* 19.13.

As a pastor, I've always been haunted by the question "If your church disappeared tomorrow, would your community miss it?" Of course, the question could be challenged because it may leave smaller churches feeling like failures or it may place too much emphasis on doing good works just to get noticed, but it still gives me pause. We want to create craters, or at least make a dent for good in our community. We hope to transform our community by bringing a temporal, relative peace that matters for eternity. We desire to plant seeds of virtue and love that blossom for eternity. For today and tomorrow, we long for God's kingdom to come and God's will to be done in our locality.

We are hopeful people—the whole Christ walking the whole journey, engaging whole persons in the whole world until we are wholly home. That's the whole story.

CONCLUSION

> For Augustine, the primary duty of the pastor is to bring the flock to Christ, the one shepherd. It is Christ who speaks and Christ who feeds, and ecclesial ministry finds its source in the good shepherd.
>
> —James K. Lee, "'One in the One Shepherd'"

> In fact, the reason why [Jesus] assumed the whole man without sin was precisely so that he could heal the whole of which man consists from the pestilence of sin.
>
> —Augustine, *The City of God* 10.27

"I want to be whole."

This is the longing of a generation broken by the fallenness of the world and the sinfulness of their own hearts.

We live in a fragmented, convulsing world. People are saddened and separated. Shame, guilt, and regret press in on people every day. For many, life feels overwhelming and meaningless.

We want to be whole.

Whole-life pastoral ministry is a holistic and hopeful journey toward healing in the whole Christ. The whole-life pastor shepherds people toward true happiness: "to cling to God as our final good, and to seek the good of our neighbor for the same end."[1]

I conclude this book with an emphasis on two summarizing descriptors of whole-life pastoral ministry: healing and humble. Whole-life ministry is healing and humble.

1. Lee, "'One in the One Shepherd,'" 236.

Healing

Whole-life pastoral ministry is healing. For Augustine, the church is better conceived as a rehabilitation center for the recovering wounded and injured than as a sports arena filled with athletes who have reached peak performance. Through the preaching of the word, the administration of the sacraments, and the practice of love, the church, as the whole Christ, is a healing community. The shepherd mercifully tends to his hurting sheep through the church. The church has not arrived but is recovering from wounds inflicted by its own transgression, the fallenness of this age, and the sins of others.

Comparing the good Samaritan to Christ and the inn to the church, Augustine writes, "Wine and oil have been poured into you, you have received the sacrament of the Only-begotten Son; you have been lifted onto his mule, you have believed that Christ became flesh; you have been brought to the inn, *you are being cured in the Church*."[2] For Augustine, the journey of healing "entailed leaving behind the pleasures of pride and complacency and learning the new pleasures of humility and love."[3]

But the complete healing of the church will not be reached in this life. This transformative process of being "conformed to the 'deep heart' of Christ" will be completed only eschatologically.[4] Thus, it is only "a gift partly received and mostly hoped for, and not in the first place an accomplishment."[5] This realistic approach "engenders a hopeful and gentle pastoral approach, for one does not need to become a member of an elite community of the sinless."[6] Thus, healing occurs in the church over time through word, sacrament, and love and will not be entirely completed until the new heaven and new earth.

By taking this therapeutic posture, we are, first, in a better position to explain why the church isn't perfect. We are not wholly whole yet. We are all in recovery and will be until Jesus Christ returns. Second, we will not pit ourselves against others or have to prove that our faith makes us superior to others. Instead, we will admit our faults and share our hurts with others as a vital part of healing their wounds. Third, we will be reminded that we are trying not to win an argument with others but to lead them to Jesus, the living shepherd and healer of our souls. Finally, we will present Jesus as a wounded healer. Jesus showed his wounds to Thomas, the skeptical disciple, so we will present Jesus

2. Augustine, *Sermons* 179a.7 (italics added).
3. Cavadini, *Visioning Augustine*, 162.
4. Cavadini, *Visioning Augustine*, 166.
5. Cavadini, *Visioning Augustine*, 141.
6. Lee, *Augustine and the Mystery of the Church*, 126. See also Lee, "'One in the One Shepherd,'" 237–39.

as a suffering savior who brings healing through his own pain. Jesus's answer to sin and suffering was not an explanation but his own woundedness. James K. A. Smith assures us, "God doesn't give us an answer; he gives us himself."[7]

Humble

As a pastor, Augustine "appeals to the mystery at the heart of the Christian faith: a humble God who endured evil in order to overcome."[8] A therapeutic approach to ministry is grounded in Jesus Christ's humility. Whole-life pastoral ministry is humble. On the occasion of a certain bishop's ordination, Augustine warns in a sermon, "Now pride is a great vice, and the first of vices, the beginning, origin and cause of all sins."[9] For Augustine, pride (*superbia*) is the seminal sin. James K. Lee offers an Augustinian theological definition of pride: "In its essence, *superbia* is the desire to replace God with oneself. It is a form of self-sufficiency that looks to oneself as the arbiter of truth and the source of delight, and thereby as the final or ultimate good. Further, pride is a failure of the imagination; it amounts to a foreclosure of vision, such that one cannot see beyond oneself."[10]

In the sermon mentioned above, Augustine uses the teaching and example of Jesus Christ to stop pride from taking root in the ordinand's future ministry. Augustine explains that by word and deed Jesus teaches pastors the way of humility. What Jesus taught and the way he lived heals our pride. Augustine emphasizes the therapeutic power of Jesus's teaching and example to cure our pride and create within us the health of humility:

- "You will remember that from the dregs of the flesh a certain appetite for superiority, for being top dog, had crept in among the disciples of our Lord Jesus Christ, our apostles, and the fumes of conceit had begun to obscure their vision. . . . The Lord, however, present *as the doctor, lanced this tumor of theirs* [using the humility of a child to teach them]."[11]
- "It is indeed by [Jesus's] blood, by his death that we have been redeemed from death, by his humility that when *we were flat on our backs we have been set on our feet.*"[12]

7. J. K. A. Smith, *On the Road*, 188.
8. J. K. A. Smith, *On the Road*, 186.
9. Augustine, *Sermons* 340a.1.
10. Lee, "'One in the One Shepherd,'" 234. Lee's article directed me to Augustine's *Sermons* 340a and helped me work through the content of the sermon.
11. Augustine, *Sermons* 340a.1 (italics added).
12. Augustine, *Sermons* 340a.3 (italics added).

- "The *great doctor came to heal our swollen condition*. From the east as far as the west the human race was lying there like *one great big invalid, and was requiring a great physician*."[13]
- "The human race was *very dangerously ill*, caught up in all sorts of vices, especially the one flowing from the source of pride; and that's why he *came to cure this pride by his own example*."[14]

In this sermon, Augustine is eloquently challenging the new bishop to serve with humility. Pride would obscure his vision of the ministry and dull his imagination, but Christ could heal him. Augustine works hard to replace images of ministry success with more humble pictures of the pastorate. Today, aspiring pastors may look to idealized ministry metaphors, such as the CEO pastor who catalyzes the growth and expansion of his megachurch or the master teacher pastor who speaks at conferences, sells books, and gets YouTube views. Augustine replaces those images with more humble metaphors grounded in Jesus's own teaching: metaphors of a servant and a child. As a servant, pastors attend to the church, not their own fame or pleasure. As a child, they realize the profound limits of their knowledge and insight. They look to the one shepherd, the source of all healing and hope.

I planted and pastored a church for fifteen years. When I decided to leave the church to become a teacher, the elders and the congregation voted to close the church. There was no controversy that had caused me to leave. No scandal. We had money in the bank and thirty acres of land that was paid for. We had no debt. The church just felt that they could not go on without me. What a colossal leadership failure on my part. I felt too much ownership of the church. I planted it and needed it to succeed. My ego and calling were wrapped up in it. I felt I needed to be in control and knew better than others—now I realize that I often did not know better. I wanted to be their hero and oftentimes felt that I was their savior. In many ways, I made the church about me. I hope I have learned my lesson. I must decrease, but he must increase. More of Jesus, less of me.

When I was asked to write a book that was more of me and less of Augustine, I was flattered but also frightened. I have seen what I can do and have come to realize that without Jesus Christ I can do nothing. I hope that this book is not primarily about Augustine or me but about Jesus Christ, our humble mediator, our healer.

Whole-life pastoral ministry recognizes that Jesus Christ is the true shepherd of the church. Pastoral ministry that makes people whole depends on

13. Augustine, *Sermons* 340a.5 (italics added).
14. Augustine, *Sermons* 340a.5 (italics added).

the whole Christ to feed the sheep. Holistic ministry that makes people whole feeds on the one Christ. Augustine makes this point in a sermon titled "On the Shepherds": "So he, the one shepherd, feeds his sheep in these [other good shepherds], and they do so in this one. . . . This is feeding Christ, this is feeding for Christ, this is feeding in Christ, not feeding oneself apart from Christ. . . . So let them all be in the one shepherd, and speak with the one voice of the shepherd which the sheep may hear and follow their shepherd, not this or that shepherd, but the one shepherd. And in him let them all speak with one voice."[15]

Truly, the whole Christ is the better pastor. And we, too, become better pastors as we shepherd others to wholeness, humbly leading them to healing in the one shepherd.

15. Augustine, *Sermons* 46.30.

POSTLUDE

"There Is a Balm in Gilead"

There is a balm in Gilead to make the wounded whole;
there is a balm in Gilead to heal the sin sick soul.

Sometimes I feel discouraged, and I think my work's in vain, but then the Holy Spirit revives my soul again.

There is a balm in Gilead to make the wounded whole;
there is a balm in Gilead to heal the sin sick soul.

If you cannot preach like Peter, if you cannot pray like Paul, you can tell the love of Jesus and say "He died for all."

There is a balm in Gilead to make the wounded whole;
there is a balm in Gilead to heal the sin sick soul.[1]

1. From *Our Great Redeemer's Praise*, 350.

BIBLIOGRAPHY

Allen, Mark. "The City of God and the City of Man." *Faith and the Academy* 6, no. 1 (2021): 8–11.

Allen, Michael. "*Totus Christus* and Praying the Psalms." *Pro Ecclesia* 29, no. 1 (2020): 45–52.

Athanasius. "A Letter of Athanasius, Our Holy Father, Archbishop of Alexandria, to Marcellinus on the Interpretation of the Psalms." In *Athanasius: The Life of Antony and the Letter to Marcellinus*, translated by Robert C. Gregg. Paulist Press, 1980.

Augustine. *The City of God (1–10)*. Edited by Boniface Ramsey. Translated by William Babcock. The Works of Saint Augustine I/6. New City, 2012.

———. *The City of God (11–22)*. Edited by Boniface Ramsey. Translated by William Babcock. The Works of Saint Augustine I/7. New City, 2013.

———. *The Confessions*. 2nd ed. Edited by John E. Rotelle. Translated by Maria Boulding. The Works of Saint Augustine I/1. New City, 2012.

———. *Confessions: A New Translation*. Translated by Sarah Ruden. Modern Library, 2017.

———. *The Enchiridion on Faith, Hope, and Charity*. In *On Christian Belief*, edited by Boniface Ramsey, translated by Bruce Herbert. The Works of Saint Augustine I/8. New City, 2005.

———. *Expositions of the Psalms 1–32*. Edited by John E. Rotelle. Translated by Maria Boulding. The Works of Saint Augustine III/15. New City, 2000.

———. *Expositions of the Psalms 33–50*. Edited by John E. Rotelle. Translated by Maria Boulding. The Works of Saint Augustine III/16. New City, 2000.

———. *Expositions of the Psalms 51–72*. Edited by John E. Rotelle. Translated by Maria Boulding. The Works of Saint Augustine III/17. New City, 2001.

———. *Expositions of the Psalms 73–98*. Edited by John E. Rotelle. Translated by Maria Boulding. The Works of Saint Augustine III/18. New City, 2002.

———. *Expositions of the Psalms 99–120*. Edited by Boniface Ramsey. Translated by Maria Boulding. The Works of Saint Augustine III/19. New City, 2003.

———. *Expositions of the Psalms 121–150*. Edited by Boniface Ramsey. Translated by Maria Boulding. The Works of Saint Augustine III/20. New City, 2004.

———. *Homilies on the First Epistle of John*. Edited by Daniel E. Doyle and Thomas Martin. Translated by Boniface Ramsey. The Works of Saint Augustine I/14. New City, 2008.

———. *Homilies on the Gospel of John 1–40*. Edited by Allen D. Fitzgerald. Translated by Edmund Hill. The Works of Saint Augustine III/12. New City, 2009.

———. *Homilies on the Gospel of John 41–124*. Edited by Allen D. Fitzgerald. Translated by Edmund Hill. The Works of Saint Augustine III/13. New City, 2020.

———. *Letters 1–99*. Edited by Boniface Ramsey. Translated by Roland Teske. The Works of Saint Augustine II/1. New City, 2001.

———. *Letters 100–155*. Edited by Boniface Ramsey. Translated by Roland Teske. The Works of Saint Augustine II/2. New City, 2003.

———. *Letters 156–210*. Edited by Boniface Ramsey. Translated by Roland Teske. The Works of Saint Augustine II/3. New City, 2004.

———. *Sermons 1–19*. Edited by John E. Rotelle. Translated by Edmund Hill. The Works of Saint Augustine III/1. New City, 1992.

———. *Sermons 20–50*. Edited by John E. Rotelle. Translated by Edmund Hill. The Works of Saint Augustine III/2. New City, 1992.

———. *Sermons 51–94*. Edited by John E. Rotelle. Translated by Edmund Hill. The Works of Saint Augustine III/3. New City, 2009.

———. *Sermons 94A–147A*. Edited by John E. Rotelle. Translated by Edmund Hill. The Works of Saint Augustine III/4. New City, 1992.

———. *Sermons 148–183*. Edited by John E. Rotelle. Translated by Edmund Hill. The Works of Saint Augustine III/5. New City, 1992.

———. *Sermons 184–229Z*. Edited by John E. Rotelle. Translated by Edmund Hill. The Works of Saint Augustine III/6. New City, 1993.

———. *Sermons 230–272B*. Edited by John E. Rotelle. Translated by Edmund Hill. The Works of Saint Augustine III/7. New City, 1993.

———. *Sermons 306–340A*. Edited by John E. Rotelle. Translated by Edmund Hill. The Works of Saint Augustine III/9. New City, 1994.

———. *Sermons 341–400*. Edited by John E. Rotelle. Translated by Edmund Hill. The Works of Saint Augustine III/10. New City, 1992.

———. *Sermons Discovered Since 1990*. Edited by John E. Rotelle. Translated by Edmund Hill. The Works of Saint Augustine III/11. New City, 1997.

———. *Teaching Christianity*. Edited by John E. Rotelle. Translated by Edmund Hill. The Works of Saint Augustine I/11. New City, 1996.

Babcock, William. Introduction to Augustine, *City of God (1–10)*.

Bates, Matthew W. *The Hermeneutics of the Apostolic Proclamation: The Center of Paul's Method of Scriptural Interpretation*. Baylor University Press, 2012.

Bavinck, Herman. *Reformed Ethics*. Vol. 1, *Created, Fallen, and Converted Humanity*. Edited by John Bolt. Baker Academic, 2019.

Berger, Peter. *The Heretical Imperative: Contemporary Possibilities of Religious Affirmation*. Doubleday, 1980.

Bonhoeffer, Dietrich. *Psalms: The Prayer Book of the Bible*. Fortress, 1970.

Bray, Gerald. *Augustine on the Christian Life: Transformed by the Power of God*. Crossway, 2015.

Brooks, David. *The Road to Character*. Random House, 2016.

Brown, Peter. *Augustine of Hippo: A Biography*. University of California Press, 1967.

Burge, Ryan P. *The Nones: Where They Came From, Who They Are, and Where They Are Going*. Fortress, 2021.

Burns, J. Patout, Jr. *Augustine's Preached Theology: Living as the Body of Christ*. Eerdmans, 2022.

Burton, Tara Isabella. *Strange Rites: New Religions for a Godless World*. Hachette Book Group, 2020.

Byassee, Jason. *Praise Seeking Understanding: Reading the Psalms with Augustine*. Eerdmans, 2007.

Calvin, John. *Commentaries on the Epistle of Paul to the Galatians and Ephesians*. Translated by William Pringle. Eerdmans, 1957.

Cameron, Michael. *Christ Meets Me Everywhere: Augustine's Early Figurative Exegesis*. Oxford University Press, 2012.

———. Introduction to *Essential Expositions of the Psalms by Saint Augustine*, edited by Boniface Ramsey, translated by Maria Boulding. New City, 2015.

Cavadini, John C. *Visioning Augustine*. Wiley-Blackwell, 2019.

Chang, Curtis. *Engaging Unbelief: A Captivating Strategy from Augustine and Aquinas*. Wipf & Stock, 2000.

Chatraw, Joshua D. *Telling a Better Story: How to Talk About God in a Skeptical Age*. Zondervan Reflective, 2020.

Chatraw, Joshua D., and Mark D. Allen. *Apologetics at the Cross: An Introduction for Christian Witness*. Zondervan Academic, 2018.

———. *The Augustine Way: Retrieving a Vision for the Church's Apologetic Witness*. Baker Academic, 2023.

———. "Preparing to Engage (Not Spin) in Later Modernism from the Inside Out." In *Apologetics at the Cross*.

Chatraw, Joshua D., and Jack Carson. *Surprised by Doubt: How Disillusionment Can Invite Us into a Deeper Faith*. Brazos, 2023.

Covey, Stephen R. "Seek First to Understand, Then to Be Understood: Principles of Emphatic Communication." In *The 7 Habits of Highly Effective People*, rev. ed. Simon & Schuster, 2020.

Elshtain, Jean Bethke. *Augustine and the Limits of Politics*. University of Notre Dame Press, 2018.

Ford, Coleman M., and Shawn J. Wilhite. *Ancient Wisdom for the Care of Souls: Learning the Art of Pastoral Ministry from the Church Fathers*. Crossway, 2024.

Harmless, William, ed. *Augustine in His Own Words*. Catholic University of America Press, 2010.

Harrison, Carol. *Augustine: Christian Truth and Fractured Humanity*. Oxford University Press, 2000.

Haykin, Michael A. G. *Amidst Us Our Beloved Stands: Recovering Sacrament in the Baptist Tradition*. Lexham, 2022.

Hays, Richard B. "Christ Prays the Psalms: Israel's Psalter as Matrix of Early Christology." In *The Conversion of the Imagination: Paul as Interpreter of Israel's Scripture*. Eerdmans, 2005.

Hendricks, Howard G., and William D. Hendricks. *Living by the Book*. Moody, 1991.

Hiestand, Gerald, and Todd Wilson. *The Pastor Theologian: Resurrecting an Ancient Vision*. Zondervan, 2015.

Holland, Tom. *Dominion: How the Christian Revolution Remade the World*. Basic Books, 2019.

Horton, Michael. "Affirming Moser's Well-Qualified *Totus Christus*." *Pro Ecclesia* 29, no. 1 (2020): 43–44.

Hunter, James Davison. *To Change the World: The Irony, Tragedy, and Possibility of Christianity in the Late Modern World*. Oxford University Press, 2010.

Johnson, Kristen Deede. *Theology, Political Theory, and Pluralism: Beyond Tolerance and Difference*. Cambridge Studies in Christian Doctrine 15. Cambridge University Press, 2007.

Jones, Timothy Paul. "Ecclesial Apologetics." In *Understanding Apologetics: Five Methods for Defending the Faith*, edited by Timothy Paul Jones. Hendrickson, 2025.

Keller, Timothy. *Center Church: Doing Balanced, Gospel-Centered Ministry in Your City*. Zondervan, 2012.

———. *Preaching: Communicating Faith in an Age of Skepticism*. Viking, 2015.

Kim, Charles G., Jr. *The Way of Humility: St. Augustine's Theology of Preaching*. Catholic University of America Press, 2023.

Kolbet, Paul R. *Augustine and the Cure of Souls: Revising a Classical Ideal*. Christianity and Judaism in Antiquity Series 17. University of Notre Dame Press, 2010.

Komline, Han-luen Kantzer. *Augustine on the Will: A Theological Account*. Oxford University Press, 2020.

Lamb, Michael. *A Commonwealth of Hope: Augustine's Political Thought*. Princeton University Press, 2022.

Lee, James K. *Augustine and the Mystery of the Church*. Fortress, 2017.

———. "'One in the One Shepherd': St. Augustine and Pastoral Ministry." *The Heythrop Journal* 63, no. 2 (2022): 232–44.

Lewis, C. S. *Mere Christianity*. Macmillan, 1952.

———. *The Weight of Glory: And Other Addresses*. Macmillan, 1980.

Lovelace, Richard F. *Dynamics of Spiritual Life: An Evangelical Theology of Renewal*. InterVarsity, 1979.

MacIntyre, Alasdair. *After Virtue: A Study in Moral Theory*. 3rd ed. University of Notre Dame Press, 2007.

Mathewes, Charles. *Books That Matter: The City of God*. Narrated by the author. Great Courses, 2016. 12 hr., 45 min.

———. "The Liberation of Questioning in Augustine's *Confessions*." *Journal of the American Academy of Religion* 70, no. 3 (2002): 539–60.

Meconi, David Vincent. *The One Christ: St. Augustine's Theology of Deification*. Catholic University of America Press, 2013.

———. *On Self-Harm, Narcissism, Atonement, and the Vulnerable Christ*. Bloomsbury, 2019.

Moser, J. David. "Corpus Mysticum: A Response to Vanhoozer, Horton, and Allen." *Pro Ecclesia* 29, no. 1 (2020): 53–67.

———. "*Totus Christus*: A Proposal for Protestant Christology and Ecclesiology." *Pro Ecclesia* 29, no. 1 (2020): 3–30.

Nouwen, Henri J. M. *In the Name of Jesus: Reflections on Christian Leadership*. Crossroad, 1989.

———. *Love, Henri: Letters on the Spiritual Life*. Edited by Gabrielle Earnshaw. Convergent, 2016.

O'Donovan, Oliver. *The Desire of the Nations: Rediscovering the Roots of Political Theology*. Cambridge University Press, 1996.

———. *Ethics as Theology*. Vol. 1, *Self, World, and Time*. Eerdmans, 2013.

———. "What Kind of Community Is the Church? The Richard Hooker Lectures 2005." *Ecclesiology* 3, no. 2 (2007): 171–93.

Pascal, Blaise. *Pascal's Pensées*. Translated by W. F. Trotter. Dutton, 1958.

———. *Pensées*. Translated by A. J. Krailsheimer. Penguin, 1995.

Pasquarello, Mike. "(#14) The Preaching Life." Presented by the Robert Smith Jr. Preaching Institute. Virtual lecture. Posted October 22, 2018, by Beeson Divinity

School at Samford University. YouTube, 23:07. https://www.youtube.com/watch?v=69m_MdNpdSc.

Peters, James R. *Logic of the Heart: Augustine, Pascal, and the Rationality of Faith.* Baker Academic, 2009.

Peterson, Eugene H. *The Contemplative Pastor: Returning to the Art of Spiritual Direction.* Eerdmans, 1989.

———. *A Long Obedience in the Same Direction: Discipleship in an Instant Society.* InterVarsity, 1980.

———. *The Pastor: A Memoir.* HarperOne, 2011.

Plato. *Charmides.* Translated by Thomas G. West and Grace Starry West. Hackett, 1986.

Plumer, Eric. *Augustine's Commentary on Galatians: Introduction, Text, Translation, and Notes.* Oxford Early Christian Studies. Oxford University Press, 2003.

Rieff, Philip. *The Triumph of the Therapeutic: The Uses of Faith After Freud.* Harper & Row, 1966. Reprint, University of Chicago Press, 1987.

Robinson, Haddon W. *Biblical Preaching: The Development and Delivery of Expository Messages.* 3rd ed. Baker Academic, 2014.

Runcorn, David. *A Center of Quiet: Hearing God When Life Is Noisy.* InterVarsity, 1990.

Schaeffer, Francis A. *Art and the Bible.* IVP Classics. InterVarsity, 2006.

Senge, Peter M. *The Fifth Discipline: The Art and Practice of the Learning Organization.* Currency Doubleday, 1990.

Senkbeil, Harold L. *The Care of Souls: Cultivating a Pastor's Heart.* Lexham, 2019.

Smith, Christian. *Soul Searching: The Religious and Spiritual Lives of American Teenagers.* With Melina Lundquist Denton. Oxford University Press, 2005.

Smith, James K. A. *Awaiting the King: Reforming Public Theology.* Vol. 3 of *Cultural Liturgies.* Baker Academic, 2017.

———. *How (Not) to Be Secular: Reading Charles Taylor.* Eerdmans, 2014.

———. *On the Road with Saint Augustine: A Real-World Spirituality for Restless Hearts.* Brazos, 2019.

———. *Who's Afraid of Postmodernism? Taking Derrida, Lyotard, and Foucault to Church.* The Church and Postmodern Culture. Baker Academic, 2007.

Taylor, Charles. *Ethics of Authenticity.* Harvard University Press, 1991.

———. *A Secular Age.* Harvard University Press, 2007.

Tennent, Timothy, and Julie Tennent. "I Have Come to Do Your Will (Psalm 40)." *Wake-Up Call* (podcast), March 16, 2025. https://seedbed.com/i-have-come-to-do-your-will-psalm-40/.

"There Is a Balm in Gilead." In *Our Great Redeemer's Praise.* Seedbed, 2022.

Vanhoozer, Kevin J. *Biblical Authority After Babel: Retrieving the Solas in the Spirit of Mere Christianity.* Brazos, 2016.

———. *The Drama of Doctrine: A Canonical Linguistic Approach to Christian Theology*. Westminster John Knox, 2005.

———. "Hocus Totus: The Elusive Wholeness of Christ." *Pro Ecclesia* 29, no. 1 (2020): 31–42.

Vanhoozer, Kevin J., and Owen Strachan. *The Pastor as Public Theologian: Reclaiming a Lost Vision*. Baker Academic, 2015.

Webster, John. *God Without Measure: Working Papers on Christian Theology*. Vol. 1, *God and the Works of God*. Bloomsbury, 2016.

Wells, Samuel. *Improvisation: The Drama of Christian Ethics*. Brazos, 2004.

Williams, Rowan. "Augustine's Christology: Its Spirituality and Rhetoric." In *In the Shadow of the Incarnation: Essays on Jesus Christ in the Early Church in Honor of Brian E. Daley, S. J.*, edited by Peter W. Martens. University of Notre Dame Press, 2008.

———. *On Augustine*. Bloomsbury, 2016.

Wright, N. T. *The Lord and His Prayer*. Eerdmans, 1996.

———. *Surprised by Hope: Rethinking Heaven, the Resurrection, and the Mission of the Church*. HarperCollins, 2008.

INDEX